Is It Just Me?

(Confessions Of An Over-Sharer)
Chrissie Swan

16

EasyRead Large

Copyright Page from the Original Book

Published by Nero,
an imprint of Schwartz Publishing Pty Ltd
37–39 Langridge Street
Collingwood VIC 3066 Australia
email: enquiries@blackincbooks.com
www.nerobooks.com

All of these columns were previously published in *Sunday Life*.

National Library of Australia Cataloguing-in-Publication entry:

Creator: Swan, Chrissie, author.
Title: Is it just me? : confessions of an over-sharer / Chrissie Swan.
Edition: Second edition.
ISBN: 9781863957519 (paperback)
ISBN: 9781922231284 (ebook)
Subjects: Anecdotes--Australia.
Australian wit and humor--21st century.
Newspapers--Sections, columns, etc.
Dewey Number: 070.4082

Cover design by Peter Long
Cover photograph by Mark Lobo

Printed in Australia by Griffin Press. The paper this book is printed on is certified
against the Forest Stewardship Council® Standards. Griffin Press holds FSC chain of
custody certification SGS-COC-005088. FSC promotes environmentally responsible,
socially beneficial and economically viable management of the world's forests.

FSC
www.fsc.org
MIX
Paper from
responsible sources
FSC® C009448

TABLE OF CONTENTS

For Christopher, Leo, Kit & Peg.
You are the stars in my sky.

Introduction

Hello and welcome to my very first book. You are smart and have wonderful taste in literature. I always liked that about you. Before I got into radio and TV I was a copywriter, which means I wrote things for advertising. I once worked with another copywriter who, on the sly, wrote proper things. He won an award for his works of fiction and my boss at the time sent around a group email lauding him for his achievements and recognition of what even he called "proper writing". The real stuff. At the agency, we loved our jobs for the grooviness and endless hilarity, but ad writing always seemed like fast food while non-fiction was like a filet mignon ... So please, dear reader, herewith find my attempt at the perfect steak. We copywriters always aspired to one day be responsible for something available in bookstores that wasn't just the catalogue so I have to admit I am proud of this little volume. I have signed a copy for myself, walked to a mirror and told myself, blushing, what a huge fan of me I was.

I am writing this to you from a table in Bali. It is the first time I have been on holiday with my three kids and partner and I have to tell you, if you are considering such a journey, that plane travel with three kids under five may well be the seventh portal of hell. I can't be sure but, yes, I think it might well be. I was supposed to write this piece two weeks ago, but between trying to get enough clothing for a family of five into one suitcase and sourcing the correct Skylanders rash vest for my four-year-old, time got away from me. So here I am. I dropped the aforementioned four-year-old in the hotel's Kids Club this morning, and when I say dropped I mean bribed and dragged. What happened to, "All kids love Kids Club"? It's a lie, that's what. My four-year-old tried it for an hour and then told me, "Why am I in there? I'm part of this holiday too, you know." So this morning I had to coax him into the big bright room heaving with happy staff and toys and paints with the promise of a Paddle Pop later on. Where I will find a Paddle Pop on this island of Bintang and braids I will never know but I'll deal with that later ... wish me luck.

When I was approached to write this weekly column I was delirious. I adored being consumed by people on Sunday morning in what I imagined was my natural habitat – surrounded by morning coffee and ruffled beds. It was sublime. I had grown used to people seeing me at the supermarket and saying they knew my work on radio and TV but there was something really super about being recognised for my writing. It made me feel so smart! I was a bit up myself about the whole thing. Mainly, that I had pulled it off and people were actually reading it. This column quickly became the favourite feather in my cap. I was very quick to update my Twitter bio to include "columnist", if you know what I mean. But by the time the first year was up I was about to give birth to my third child, a baby girl named Peggy, and I had never felt older or more tired. I felt like one of those Italian miracle mothers who conceive at sixty-five. I was shuffling around like my pelvis was made of balsa wood and I couldn't bear to look at my diary. My friend had recently introduced me to an app on my phone which beeped every time I had to be somewhere ... the obstetrician, a radio planning session, a TV production meeting, a flight interstate to film my TV show, an orientation day for a kindergarten, and every time it clanged I wanted to cry/throw it against the wall/make another cup of coffee. Needless to say, I drank a lot of coffee. But something had to give so I made the grown-up decision of stepping away from the column for a while. My dad always told me to quit while I was ahead. But he also said, "Make hay while the sun shines," so I'm pretty sure he was put on this earth to vex and confuse me with philosophical sayings. Besides, with two radio shows, a prime-time TV show, a column and three little kids (none at school yet), I figured I'd gathered enough bloody hay, thank you very much. As if I wasn't busy enough I decided to sell the family home and move into another one as well. Easy on the hay now, lady. Step away from the hay for Chrissakes. YOU HAVE ENOUGH HAY.

It was, as you can imagine, a very busy time. But I always found an hour or so to sneak away and write these columns every week. My mum would watch the kids and I would haul my not unsubstantial bottom across a local park, plop myself under the tree and start writing. If these pages were scratch-and-sniff they would smell of grass clippings and sunshine and the occasional surprise sprinkler. I have loved sharing my bits and pieces with you. And if you have only read a few before, or if you haven't read any of them at all, here they are. The one about never having nookie, the one about kangaroo tail stew, the one about my great regret about not being born Greek, the one about my fabulous sisters ... And even a few that got me into all sorts of trouble in the press, inspiring people to be cruel and sending me to a car wash to weep uncontrollably in private. They're all here. Rightly or wrongly. Because surely, I can't be the only one asking ... is it just me?

Relight my fire

I can count on one hand the number of times I've slept with my partner in the past six months. Let's be honest, I can count on three fingers. This isn't good enough but I just don't feel like it. I have a seven-month-old, a three-year-old and several jobs and, frankly, I'm busy. But lots of people have kids and jobs and the world continues to get populated. What's wrong with me?

Lately, I have even been known to actively avoid a dalliance. I confess I have perfected the exact breathing pattern that gives my fella the idea I'm already asleep when he comes a-callin'. I learnt this method from that scene in *Ferris Bueller's Day Off* where Ferris tricks his mum into thinking he's still in bed by using an elaborate sound recording of snores and splutters, when actually he's on a float in town singing "Twist and Shout". See? Who said Matthew Broderick never taught us anything?

I never thought this would be me. Five years ago our lerve was as fresh as a pack of hot cross buns. Steamy. I'd kiss my partner at every red light. I remember the first time he held my hand. I'd broken a pair of thongs and as we crossed a road he slipped his big man-paw into mine and the world stopped. Truth be told, it still stops when he holds my hand today. But it's always so brief because mine has to fly out within ten seconds to catch a runaway stroller/mouthful of organic rice cereal/Buzz Lightyear hurtling from hands of three-year-old towards temple of baby.

Last week I caught up with a girlfriend who's also lacking a bit in the fornication stakes. She'd read about a thirty-day challenge where couples pledge to make sweet love every day for a month. She and her husband had given it a go despite having five-year-old twins and a nine-year-old, and only made it to day seventeen. She seemed deflated by her failure until I confessed that what her husband had got in just over two weeks was what my man could expect over a period of three years.

And so we decided over two flat whites and a Portuguese tart that I'd have a crack, too. So I started Operation Common-Law Wife Duty Fulfilment. The first night, I had a shower, squirted on some aromatics and loitered with intent. This involved laying myself out on our bed, Barbara Cartland-style, in a new nightie I got from Myer in a "30 per cent off already reduced red-ticketed items" sale. In the end it cost me $7.13, so I was lusty AND thrifty. A potent combination. Truthfully, it was quite nice to be boudoir-ready before the onset of what I like to call the "zombie zone". That's the time of the evening when I'm sitting slack-jawed on the sofa, with my head rolled back, begging my boyfriend to drag me up the hallway on a blanket, like a removalist with a piano.

So we're in bed. Smelling like a mistress from the '80s and wearing a shop-soiled size-20 negligee. The first thing he does when he joins me is chuckle a bit under his breath. I ask him, "Ummm ... why are you laughing? Can't you see I've gone to the effort of coming to bed tonight theme-dressed as Sally Spectra [from *The Bold and the Beautiful*] ?"

"No," he says. "I just had a flash of you today when that bird flew into the kitchen and that sound you made." Earlier that day, an Indian myna had maliciously hopped in through an open window and flapped about the kitchen. I have a terrible phobia about birds. The following five minutes involved me waving a broomstick, calling for my kids to run and hide and yelling at my man to stop convulsing with laughter and help me.

So, despite my efforts on night number one of Operation Common-Law Wife Duty Fulfilment, it turned out that both of us, by the light of our charging iPhones, laughed so hard we woke the baby. On night number two we guffawed about our three-year-old's obsession with the fold-out sofa he calls his nest. On night number three I had to tell him to stop talking about the time he was cornered by an acquaintance at a cafe and had a whole conversation with a cappuccino dripping off his beard. And so on.

I realised that going to bed early had given us these top-shelf moments. We could never have done this five years ago, because we hadn't done the time. To be physical together is lovely and necessary (and I've taken care of that, if you know what I mean) but the practice of getting into bed before we're written off for the day had given us the opportunity for what I realised is real intimacy. I had to take the exact steps we took when we first met all those years ago. We talked. Then we laughed. Then we got it on.

So my advice is, sure, get all Barbara Cartland with your perfume and saucy outfits, but don't jump straight to the end of the book – because all the good stuff is in chapter one.

25th March 2012

I kissed a Chiko Rolland I liked it

I am overweight and happy. It hasn't always been this way. I mean, I've always been "happy", but I've lived with the dream of a "goal weight" hanging in front of me like a carrot (cake) since I was about eleven years old.

I recently found a diary entry from when I was twelve: "I'm going on holiday and I hope to lose weight but I'm not telling anyone so it'll be a surprise." At that time I was cutting the crusts off my Bornhoffen toast (half the calories of toast are in the crust) and spreading it with whipped margarine (whipped with air – no calories in air). How miserable.

As I grew older I believed if I arrived at this fabled "goal weight", then my life would be better. I'd be the sort of person who laughed loud during long lunches with beautiful friends. I'd have a string of handsome suitors and go on great road trips.

In the meantime I'd wait and starve and count calories. I was permanently on hold. I had boyfriends and flings but none were any good. I blamed my weight. If I was at my "goal weight" I'd find someone amazing and we'd drive to places for weekends away and listen to Nick Drake. Instead, I was heavy and this was why, as my friend so aptly put it, I was a "turd magnet". Thin people had great boyfriends, didn't everyone know that?

When I met my partner I was wearing a size-20 dress and I was at a pub. It was summer and after three weeks of dating he made me a mixtape and track three was by Nick Drake. We quickly organised a spur-of-the-moment week in New Zealand. Hold on ... isn't this the sort of beautiful life reserved only for people at their goal weight?

Then I had babies. Confidence and respect for my body soared. This body, so imperfect and so far from its "goal weight", had created human beings. These human beings loved my body. My body was needed. What's more, I realised it was a perfectly good body.

About two years ago I decided I was tired of waiting to live. What if I never got to my "goal weight"? I would have spent my whole life waiting. What a waste.

So I like the idea of living the kind of life you want ... right now. I started putting my runners in the car so I could go for a walk whenever I wanted. This is the sort of thing I thought Goal Weight Chrissie would do. Goal Weight Chrissie would go to the beach with her kids and build sandcastles. So that's what I do. Goal Weight Chrissie would eat big bowls of fresh salad and small bowls of delicious cheese. So that's what I do.

Being overweight is not easy. Normal-sized people like to talk about statistics so diabolical it's a wonder we even see any chubby people at all: we should all have exploded from some cardiac-related disease years ago.

Do-gooders look at us with concerned eyes and talk about blood pressure, circulation, difficulty conceiving ... the list goes on. I can only talk for myself and say that yes, I am overweight, but my blood pressure is normal (to low), my circulation is great, I am not pre-diabetic (or pre-anything) and I conceived two children (one while I was on the Pill and the other after four days of thinking "Hmm, maybe a second baby would be nice...").

There's no doubt overweight people can have problems conceiving. But so does my size-10 friend. No body, fat or thin, is without its issues. It's more about the type of life you're living. I eat well, grow a lot of my own food and cook 99 per cent of the food I eat. Processed food and creepy ingredients aren't good for you, no matter what size you are.

Life as an overweight woman is an exercise in apology. You always feel like you have to say sorry for your presence. That's what those sad eyes on the awkward size-18 waitress are saying: "Sorry you have to see me."

If you eat in public, you leave yourself open to screaming voices from cars. It doesn't matter if you're eating a salad roll on the way to a meeting, and God help you if it's a Chiko roll. If you must go to a drive-thru, to make sure the attendants realise you're ordering for a group and don't think the four burgers are just for you, you end up saying things like, "Let me see ... Sam wanted a Big Mac meal, didn't he?" (I'm cringing writing this because I'm guilty of it all.)

Ordering a full-cream flat white is often met with judgmental eyes, yet people at their "goal weight" do it every day of the week. So I do it, too. I'm not ashamed any more. It's satisfying to tuck into a California roll in full view of strangers.

I'm tired of maligning my size. So while I come to terms with my super-disobedient body that refuses to get thin despite pictures of Kate Winslet on my vision board, I refuse to put joy on hold for a time that may never come. I'm ordering that flat white and enjoying it. You should, too. Your Goal Weight Self would want it that way.

1st April 2012

Friends these days

When I was growing up Catholic the nuns used to make us sing a song called "Friends Are like Flowers". It seemed sweet enough, posing questions like, "Are you a daisy, a rose or a dandelion?"

Incidentally, I don't think I'd like to be any of those floral examples. Daisy: boring. Rose: pretty, but nasty. Dandelion: hollow and likely to skedaddle in a thousand directions at the first sign of trouble.

I have a friend who is fleshy and Dutch. She'd be a tulip. That's a no-brainer. But what kind of flower represents the infectious hilarity of my friend who calls his mouth the "food-hole" and took my old corgi cross out for a nightcap? Or the sassiness of one gal pal who, in her newly single twenties, would lay back in her bed after she'd finished with her prey and point a languid finger to a Post-it note with the number of a taxi service on it (no words, just that languid finger)?

And what of my best friend, to whom no flower could ever do justice? There's just not a floral equivalent of her loyalty, quirkiness and empathy.

Sure, my friends come in all sorts of colours and often arrive at my place in bunches, but that's where the similarity to flowers ends.

I'm not proud to confess that, as my life has become fuller, my gang of friends has become smaller. Wilted. I never wanted this to happen. I just sort of looked up one day and they'd shuffled away. I have a small clutch of stayers – friends who still want to talk to me about my vegie patch/penchant for burnt-fig ice-cream/need for enormous handbags, but the truth is, I'm kinda boring. I probably would've stopped answering my calls, too. I spend all my time at the radio station, at home (I like to call it "The Compound") with my kids or doing important stuff like driving to strangers' houses in suburbs I've never heard of to pick up bouncinettes, ExerSaucers and vintage school desks from eBay that are "pick-up only". You know, all the important things.

I actually used to be a really top-notch friend. Ten years ago BC (before children), my ground-floor apartment in a groovy inner city cul-de-sac was home to great parties, generous home-cooked feeds and smoky all-night gabfests. I liked to lay it all on – so much that I had to cut back from bottles to casks ... you know, so I could make the rent. My friends were beloved. And I saw so much of them! A few times a week we'd meet to tear strips off a reality TV show together or spin the lazy Susan at our local Chinese restaurant. These days I'm lucky to tap out a text once a week. And I'm actually okay with that.

I mean, sure, I miss the no-holds-barred fun I used to have with my old friends. But the fact is, the person I was ten years ago would have nothing in common with the person I am today, and the same probably applies to those friends who have moved on from me for more interesting pastures. The 28-year-old Chrissie would be bored stiff with my current chatter about variable interest rates and Leo calling his little Casio piano keyboard his "punano". I'm bored just thinking about it. I'm drooping. Someone please cut my stem and empty one of those sachets in my water.

No. Friends are not like flowers. Friends are, I have come to the conclusion, more like diners. And my life is the restaurant.

When my social life was new and shiny and freshly open for business, you could get a table without a booking and just walk in off the street. I was cheap and cheerful and definitely BYO. Sure! Bring your friends, I'll squeeze them in. Over the years the restaurant has certainly become busier. Getting a table is much harder now. Some days the blinds stay shut. All. Day. Long.

I have regular customers who eat here every single day. My family. And their tables are just not up for grabs. Ever. But still, there are the good tables by the window and they're reserved for the small group of smiley diners who've been around since opening night. For some reason they keep coming back to my restaurant, even though the service is hit-and-miss and the food is often uninspired (or burnt, or made by the clever Indian fellow down the road and passed off as my own).

Yep. And still they come, seemingly oblivious to the fact that the bonkers maître d' has a Farex-encrusted cardigan and doesn't stop banging on about her vegie patch and burnt-fig ice-cream and her need for enormous handbags.

8th April 2012

Logies vs Lego

On Logies night I will be swapping my usual Sunday-evening attire of a leopard-print Snuggie and mismatched sports socks for a shiny navy gown. I've scored an invitation to the Logies – TV's "night of nights" – and, truth be told, it's a gorgeous evening, so it's nice to have "an airing", as Gran used to say.

As you can imagine, the transition from a Sunday night spent watching *60 Minutes* and trawling Coles Online to trundling up a red carpet in borrowed jewels and a pinchy wedge heel is not the easiest thing to pull off with two tiny children and two jobs.

A little while ago I was approached to be in a glossy magazine article about my Logies prep. They imagined a four-page spread highlighting the treatments, pills and potions I invest in weeks before the ceremony. Much to their disappointment, I told them they could probably fit this exposé on the contents page, as my preparation involves roughly three steps: get a dress; put it on; go to Logies.

Actually, that's a lie. I do squeeze in a nice bouncy blow wave, too. Best $50 a gal can spend and I do like big hair – it goes with the rest of me. The glossy went with Jessica Marais in the end, I think. Wise choice all round.

In 2011 I got in super-early with a Logies frock I'd bought online for $39.95. Simple. Black. Some lace. I think there was a satin bow in there somewhere. It was a little bit Miss Piggy meets *The Godfather,* which was, quite frankly, exactly the look I was after. But then I was nominated for three individual awards and one for *The Circle* and things got nuts. Really nuts. A dressmaker was flown from interstate to measure me up and I ended up with an amazing dress with more feathers and bones than a gaggle of geese. You don't remember it? There's a Google search in it for you.

I won the Most Popular New Female Talent award, which made me feel very young. And also very proud. It is an enormous honour to think that thousands of people voted for little old me. I still look at the Logie a few times a week (it's on my mantelpiece out of the reach of my three-year-old after the time I found it in the garden buried up to its neck) and get a little rush. Its glorious presence more than makes up for the crushing disappointment I felt when I didn't make prefect and came fifteenth in the 1987 Westpac Mathematics Competition.

This year I am nominated again for a silver statuette, which came as a complete surprise but certainly a pleasant one. When I left *The Circle* in 2011 to spend more time with my two little boys, a part of me mourned the loss of showbiz and all its shininess. That job was a dream come true. In saying "yes" to more time chiselling hardened Play-Doh off my kitchen floor, I said "no" to daily guffaws with my on-air girlfriends, permanently killer hair and an abundance of free stuff. Could there be a greater luxury than someone quietly placing a strong flat white at your elbow while you type your notes into an autocue?

The decision to leave was tough but something had to give. I returned to full-time work eight weeks after my second child was born in August 2011, and during the last few months of that year I somehow managed to keep a newborn breastfed baby alive, herd a toddler and, along with my beautiful and supportive co-hosts, churn out more live TV than any other show on Network Ten. I'd done it with one kid but doing it with two was a different ball game. I actually barely remember that time. I do remember, though, that some days I had to consciously stop and focus all my concentration just to remember how to put the car in drive. When I started thinking I should have had fewer children, I knew I was out of balance. And possibly out of my mind.

I have always loved to work. But then I had children and nothing could have prepared me for how much I love being their mother. I've heard people say parenting is the hardest job in the world but to me it is pure joy. But it does take time – something I just didn't have. Luckily the choice was there for me to switch to breakfast radio, which sees me home before my three-year-old, Leo, is tucking into his morning-tea blueberries. And to afford those, I sell homemade lemonade from my driveway on weekends

– have you seen the price of those things? I'm surprised they're not delivered from the market in an Armaguard van, just like the winning Logies envelopes.

Tonight I'm getting a hairdo, whacking on a shiny new frock and sharing some laughs with my friends Gorgi Coghlan, Yumi Stynes, Denise Drysdale and Pam Barnes. I'll be the one in navy, thrilled to bits to be on the red carpet. And instead of all the worry associated with borrowing thousands of dollars worth of diamonds, I'll stick two new-season blueberries on my earlobes. I'll be sure to wave.

15th April 2012

Not the loneliest number

Yesterday I had lunch with a big gang of my old colleagues. They're a groovy and sunny bunch of twenty-somethings. One of my favourites, Xavier, told me that since we'd last seen each other he'd moved from an inner-city share house to his own seventh-floor beachside apartment. By his own admission, the rent was so high he couldn't afford to eat but, he said, it was worth it. I got a faraway look in my eye. Imagining Xavier. In his apartment. Alone. Doing nothing.

And I got nostalgic for aloneness. I have about fifteen minutes a day where I am truly alone, and that is when I'm in the car on the way to work at 5am. I really miss being alone. I miss time. I can't even go to the bathroom uninterrupted. In fact, as I write this piece, one of my "housemates" has taken a break from collecting keys in his trike basket and is prodding my foot every five seconds or so with a pair of kid-safe scissors. It may come as no surprise that this is supremely annoying. This never happened in the good old days when I happily ticked the "spinster" category on the census form.

More Australians than ever before are living alone, and before you're quick to conjure images of overweight, bearded ladies with cats, eating out of open cans on the ironing board, consider the figure of almost one in four. Yep. A whole quarter of the population are returning home to find the kitchen exactly as they left it.

So why do we feel so sorry for them? People who live alone say they often feel marginalised and looked upon with pity as they have yet to hit the conventional "life jackpot" of partner/kids/someone to steer the Winnebago with. My gran lived to be eighty-six and never remarried after her husband passed away when she was only fifty-one. That's thirty-five years of meals for one. When I asked her why she never hooked up again, she said, "Why the hell would I want to do that?"

Living alone seems to be the ultimate in thumbing your nose at society. To live your own life and be accountable only to yourself is to shirk the responsibility of becoming a wife/mother or husband/father. What happens to people who don't want these titles?

Ten years ago, I was living alone with two cats and loving it. If my nearest and dearest were worried, they never said anything to me about it but, then again, I was probably too busy arranging my CDs in alphabetical order or high-fiving my gran to notice. I have always loved living alone. As soon as I could, I moved into my own place. I'd cook and organise and nap and read the newspaper cover to cover. I fell completely in love with who I was.

I also liked how being alone allowed me to truly be myself. Who could be mad at the wet towels on the bathroom floor? Or dinners consisting only of brown rice and tuna? Or watching back-to-back episodes of *Survivor?* No one, that's who. Bliss! I spent many a cask wine–fuelled evening in the then-revolutionary "chat rooms", just to see what was doing.

I was mad for it. It didn't matter that a simple conversation consisting of "Hi, how are you? What do you do for a living?" took about forty-five minutes via dial-up modem, being in the midst of it let me feel as if I was at Central Perk from *Friends,* without even having to put a bra on.

I worry that if I hadn't been plucked from my singular existence, it would only have been a matter of time before emergency crews were fighting through stacks of newspapers and stockpiled tins of chickpeas, before realising that the only way to get me out was via cherry picker. If you are lucky enough to enjoy your own company, living alone can be a slippery slope to Hermitville, population: you. Having no one to answer to and be responsible for can be as addictive as crack cocaine and, as anyone footing the rent for a one-bedroom inner-city apartment will attest, just as expensive.

Living with people (my partner and two little ones) means I have to keep myself nice and live like a normal person. But sometimes I crave the good old days and I get jealous of those who have a little flat somewhere and a car with no baby seats in it. Those living that life right now should enjoy every minute because chances are it won't last.

One day, like me, you'll find yourself begging your tiny housemate for some privacy, with aforementioned housemate alleviating your distress with questions like, "Will a laser beam help?"

22nd April 2012

The other woman

Most of us are good, most of the time. Apart from the person who invented the Milk & Cookies Milky Bar, who is inherently evil.

I like to believe that people are generally wonderful. But sometimes good people do bad things. Like me, for example. When I was in my late twenties, I was the other woman. Now, before you tear up this book and strike me off your Christmas-card list, please consider that it was a total accident.

I had met a charming lawyer – let's call him Matt – at a barbecue and we had hit it off like a Weber on fire over a few sausages-in-bread and a nifty pasta salad. Matt lived in the country, which was great for me as I wasn't up for a full-on relationship that involved spending nights on the couch in trackies watching *Hey Hey It's Saturday.* I didn't want boring and I certainly didn't get it.

Things progressed quickly and, between my job as an advertising copywriter and my fabulous single life I enjoyed with my naughty friends, we'd meet at my flat, which resembled a two-storey garage, for clandestine grease-and-oil changes. It was, to say the least, exciting. But it never occurred to me to ask why he'd always answer my calls (only ever to his mobile – alarm bell number one: no home phone) within the first ring and there was never a chance to leave a voicemail message. Ever. He didn't have the option (alarm bell number two: no voicemail). It would just ring out.

One night I was at a friend's party and I had a missed call from a private number, which I knew would be him (alarm bell number three: silent numbers). I excused myself from the third round of Midori Shakers and called him back from outside the pub – only to be surprised when a voicemail message kicked in. "Hi! You've called Dave ... and Clare.[1] If you have an inquiry about your tax return something something something..." I didn't hear the end of the MessageBank greeting because I'd passed out in the gutter. Or maybe it was the sound like a kettle whistling on my eardrum that muffled the end of it.

He was married. His name wasn't Matt. He was an accountant. The single lawyer called Matt I'd been seeing for a few months was actually a married accountant called Dave. Ten minutes later, he called me back after having seen two missed calls from me. Clearly oblivious to the fact he'd activated his identity-revealing voicemail greeting, the conversation started cheerily enough.

Matt/Dave: "Hey, gorgeous! Are you having a good night?"

---

[1] All names have been changed.

Chrissie/Idiot: "Yeah. It's all right ... but not as exciting as hanging out with a married accountant called Dave."

Matt/Dave: *Click.*

He must have hit a weird reception patch or gone through a tunnel. At home. Because his phone immediately dropped out. And I never called again. I really wanted to. Because I wanted the nitty-gritty. I was sleepless with questions. How did he decide to do this? Had he done it before? Was I a moron? How many others had been hoodwinked? Did his wife know? Could he do me a good deal on my tax return?

I'd have vivid dreams where I'd confront him and abuse him with clever arguments for which he had no answers. The lack of closure sent me mad. Armed with his true identity, profession and the town he lived in (the only piece of his story that checked out), I was able to track him down and see where he lived and worked. And I drove there.

Before you start calling Glenn Close's management and asking her to play me in a biopic, consider that I really had no clue as to why I was in the car with the street directory opened on a page with lots of white and green bits leading me down a highway I'd never been on to a place I'd never heard of. I think I just wanted to see something real.

I got to his street and drove past his house, where a pretty blonde was helping two kids out of a car. So there were kids, too. I didn't see that coming. It made me so sad for them. What sort of a man was this? I contemplated doing a U-turn and telling her to run. That her husband was a liar and a narcissist and perhaps her whole life was a lie. But it wasn't really my place, was it? I drove away.

To this day I wonder if that was the right thing. Would I want to know if my husband had been up to this? I care deeply about the sisterhood and would do nothing to make a woman and mother question what she believed was true and real in her life. But does keeping her husband's secret make me complicit? Or should I have told her and watched what meant nothing to me and nothing to anyone, in the scheme of things, destroy the lives of many?

29th April 2012

I need help

Last week my friend called me out on something I've been doing for about three years. I thought no one had noticed my hoodwinking habit, but I was wrong, apparently. I'm blushing now as I write this, as I undoubtedly did then, when she said, "Why do you call your nanny your babysitter?"

"Do I? Really? I don't. Do I? Really? Do I?"

"Yeah, you do. You always have. It's fine ... but I was just wondering ... why?"

Again I said I wasn't even aware I did it. But I was aware. Am aware. I've been doing it on purpose so people don't get the wrong idea about the way I live and start to assume I'm clapping my hands twice to clear the table when I've finished my caviar and complaining to Raoul about the leaves in the pool.

The fact is, I work in breakfast radio, which means I have to skulk out of the house like a one-night stand before dawn every day. I've exited this way for more than five years. My partner also works and has to be on site with his little blue Esky of Yoplait tubs and ham sangas by 7am. Like clockwork, at 6.20am three mornings a week, Kirsty arrives at our house in a cloud of Clinique, happy to love my children while we're out earning enough money to keep a roof over all of our heads. She has been coming for nearly three years. In our absence, she cuddles our children and calls them gorgeous and doesn't seem to mind the world's biggest three-year-old crashing into her like a cheesy AWF wrestler.

Kirsty is, and has been for a while, a nanny. But I have always referred to her as a babysitter because everyone knows that nannies are for rich people who are too busy playing tennis and having long and late liquid lunches to be bothered raising their own children. To have a babysitter is far more egalitarian. And a lot less up yourself.

My life, as a working mother of two small boys, is busy. I simply can't pull it all off without help. To assume that anyone can is completely bonkers. So why are we lying about getting help? I lie because I get the distinct vibe that I am perceived as being selfish for working; that work is somehow a luxury I have chosen over raising my children, and I am fist-pumping the air every time I pull out of the driveway, screaming, "See ya later, suckers!" over my shoulder. Which, on occasion, I have done. But usually I am quietly frowning and trying to distract myself from the memory of my warm, curly-headed babies all chubby in their beds as I swoosh through green lights listening to the 4.30am news.

There is also the perception that if I'm going to be bold enough to work, I should bloody well do all the housework myself, at the very least. Well, I don't. I'm outing myself. I have a cleaner, Rita. She comes for two hours on a Monday and it is the highlight of my week. For about an hour, before Leo gets home from kindergarten, my house is shining. As opposed to *The Shining,* which is more like it is when Leo gets home. I can't mop my floors with two kids running, riding or crawling all over it all the time! Why do I feel bad about getting someone to do it in the only two hours in a week when there's no one in the house? Why am I even justifying it now to you?

I'm justifying it because we are supposed to be doing it all and doing it easily. If we have put our careers on hold to raise our kids at home, we'd better have a great sex life, nutritious meals on the table every night and a house so clean and stylish it could have been torn from the pages of *Vogue Living.* If we're working, we'd better not let that affect our ability to rival Samantha from '60s sitcom *Bewitched* in the wife/mother/housekeeper stakes.

What a load of tosh. I'm here to tell you it's okay to ask for help. And it's okay to pay for it, too. Whether you're working or not. The fact that you have a nanny or a cleaner doesn't mean you're living high on the hog. It doesn't mean your life is easy.

And it doesn't mean you're up yourself, either. It simply means you like clean floors and would prefer your kids weren't left at home alone to turn your place into something from *Lord of the Flies.*

Today I've outed myself as having a nanny and a cleaner. I think I'm on a roll! You know what else? I have my milk delivered (free!) every Friday. I use Coles Online so I can do the weekly shopping in front of *The Voice* AND I don't have to carry it up the front steps. And what about this? Clem at my fruit shop has generously offered free delivery of our weekly fresh bits. I've accepted. Finally, here's the big one. The biggest shortcut. The greatest up-yourself extravagance in my entire life. Instead of dishwashing powder, I. Buy. Finish. Powerballs. Gee, that feels good!

6th May 2012

Road trip

Aaahhhh! Holidays. Is there anything more exciting than that trip up the freeway to the long-term car park at the airport? The delicious panic of wondering if you've packed an extra camera battery and the feverish checking that your passport is still safe in its purpose-bought bag you hunted down at the travel shop?

I have had a few such holidays in my time. First, I went to Tokyo to teach English when I was eighteen. It was a working holiday and my first trip overseas on my own. Upon my arrival at Narita airport, if you listened closely, you could hear the popping of new pathways being blown in my brain. The smells, people – even the cabs – were worlds away from what I had been accustomed to: namely the comfort of eating spag bol in my mother's mission-brown kitchen and weekends spent watching *Countdown Revolution.*

In Tokyo, as a young lass, I met a fellow expat. In hindsight, he looked not dissimilar to Elton John, but to my teenage eyes he was laconic and handsome and older. He barely knew I existed and after a few months of my desperate flirting, he introduced me to his lithe Japanese girlfriend.

More than ten years later, I took another working holiday, this time to Jakarta for just over a year. I accepted a position as creative director of an ad agency in the bustling capital. I was lured by the promise of a salary in US dollars and the inclusion of a driver and a maid. What I learnt was that no amount of perceived luxury can replace the ability to walk down to your local for a flat white or enjoy a drink in a hotel bar without the risk of being blown up. I also missed taking in big lungfuls of air without getting two black rings of motorbike-exhaust residue around my nostrils. I couldn't get home fast enough.

In 2007, the year before we started our family, my man, The Chippie, and I visited a little town called Waitomo, which is about 200 kilometres south of Auckland. It is where you'll find a hotel that is three parts Fawlty Towers and one part the Overlook Hotel from *The Shining.* The natty fellow who checked us in also carried our luggage, turned down the beds, delivered room service and served our chowder in the dining room. I think I also saw him driving a golf buggy and pruning shrubs. He may or may not have been the ghost who allegedly haunted the bell tower.

Aside from hosting the world's spookiest hotel, Waitomo is also home to glow-worm caves. To see them you have to get on a boat like one from Willy Wonka's chocolate factory, and glide silently on an icy underground river. In the echoey blackness, you look up and there are billions of flickering glow-worms.

I'd never seen anything like it, and when I did, I wept hot little tears of joy. The sight was breathtaking, but more than that, there was something about being newly in love and overseas, knowing I was loved in return and experiencing life at its simplest and best, that made that moment unforgettable.

Later, when we'd had our first baby, we took off for a week to Tasmania. It was the winter of 2009 and Leo was about eight months. We took the boat across so we could bring our car and the roughly seventeen tonnes of kid stuff we required for the seven-day trip. We took a full-size infant bath. And a bottle steriliser the size of a Volkswagen. We also packed about 45,000 nappies because, Lord knows, there are no nappies in Tassie.

We trundled from scenic lookout to bric-a-brac stall to the twenty-eighth colonial jail in a four-kilometre radius, and I sat in a gutter outside Hobart's Salamanca Market feeding Leo from a jar of something while he sat in his car seat. It might not sound like much, but it was a brilliant shake-up from our usual structured mealtimes and home-made organic food.

On that holiday, Leo decided he was over his dummy and learnt to sleep unswaddled. There is something about being away from familiar routines that forces fabulous things to occur, and everyone benefits. Even babies.

In fact, all sorts of magic happens on holidays. Travel is life-changing and when you build memories, you enrich your life. And it doesn't seem to matter if your pilgrimage is to Floriade or fancy Florence – as long as you're on the road, it feels as if you're really living.

Your bed may be akin to an oversize phone book and the food might nearly kill you, but isn't it great?

But right now I'm feeling that what would enrich my life is a week poolside in Bali with magazines and a do-not-disturb doorknob tag. Two questions: 1. How much would the excess baggage be for a trike, ExerSaucer and Jolly Jumper? And 2. Does anyone know somewhere with a good kids' club?

20th May 2012

Work for that dream job

Last month, I was lucky enough to interview my foodie hero, Heston Blumenthal. He has a restaurant just west of London called The Fat Duck, which serves up tricky meals such as desserts that look like fried eggs and cakes that are actually chicken liver pâté. He's a clever fellow and his TV show gets a good going over at Chez Chrissie.

I've always liked the cut of his jib, and even more so after doing a little research and finding out that not only is he self-taught and one of only three Britons to achieve Michelin three-star status, he also did his fair share of crappy jobs – including that of a photocopier salesman and debt collector. It cemented my belief that terrible jobs are good for you.

At thirty-eight, I have achieved a kind of career nirvana. I work in radio, which works well with my maternal commitments and allows me to talk at length about issues ranging from *The Voice* to breastfeeding. I adore it. I also work in TV, which means I get to have fun and a free hairdo. But these jobs were a long time coming. Before I got so lucky, I submitted my tax file number to a number of positions, ranging from less than desirable to downright dehumanising. And I'd do them all again. Because they were good for me.

When I was nineteen, I deferred from uni and worked fulltime in a supermarket deli. Among other things, this involved defrosting boxes of frozen chickens, removing their necks (secreted within the carcass) and rodding them up on giant skewers to be roasted. Rivulets of pale-pink liquid would run down my inner arm and into my undergarments, heating up over the course of my shift and threatening to produce some kind of salmonella stock. The upside of this job was that, to this day, I really know my *presswurst* from my *pariser;* the downside was that I feel enormous guilt when I ask for thinly sliced anything. Such a hassle.

I've also been a manager of a clothes shop. I loved the 30 per cent off everything in-store, but wasn't such a fan of the constant sweeping of mountains of fluff out of changing rooms fogged in foot odour.

I've also arrived at a smoky office block (back when you could smoke at work) and settled in with a dial-up phone to cold-call strangers, selling them window treatments that turned perfectly good houses into soundproof yet inescapable prisons. Now that was a tough gig. I have also been a call-centre rep for a New Zealand electricity company, a mobile DJ and a showground ice-cream seller.

It wasn't until I worked for free, though, that I started achieving my career dreams. While I was studying advertising at uni, the staff made an entire class out of warning us about how hard it was to get a job in the profession we were sinking ourselves into HECS debt to become qualified for. We'd be lucky to get work in a suburban agency writing copy for instruction manuals, let alone an amazing gig with a corner office working on blue-chip accounts, like Darrin's on *Bewitched.*

With a vast history of ordinary jobs, I had only one thing left to do. I contacted a groovy inner-city ad agency and offered my services for free. They accepted and I found myself scooting into the agency between lectures and tutes to write press ads for a department store. The first ad I ever wrote was five words saying that a new store had opened. I still have it. And it still gives me a thrill.

I was so enamoured with the industry that I started skipping class so I could talk layouts and fonts and deadlines. Eventually, I quit uni and started a proper paid job as a copywriter for another outfit – but what got me the role was the experience I'd gained at that groovy inner-city agency. I am eternally grateful to whoever it was that gave a friendly 24-year-old with a bad moustache a go. And, wherever possible, I try to return the favour by giving work-experience kids the time of day and considering the whole person, not just the qualification, for a position.

Today's workplaces are so busy and often understaffed. The sad fact is that sometimes it is disruptive to the routine to make room for a young person who just wants a chance. The temptation to throw applications for work experience or internships straight into the bin without even opening them is great.

We might think that there wouldn't be a person alive who'd want to hang out in our office, do the lunch run and photocopy those proposals. But we'd be wrong. My bet is there are loads of twenty-somethings who'd be hanging out just to see what your tea room looks like.

And if you're one of those twenty-somethings wondering how you're going to break into your dream job, wax up your mo and write that letter. Who knows where it will lead you?

27th May 2012

Weighing up children

My three-year-old is seven kilos overweight. This might not sound like much, but for a preschooler, this is a big deal. I'd noticed he'd started getting larger in the past twelve months. Looking at photos of him taken this time last year showed a huge difference in appearance.

Sure, he'd grown taller. He'd had his first proper haircut where his cherubic blond curls had been snipped away to reveal a very serious and surprisingly dark businessman's hairdo. But his baby softness had gone, too. In its place was a little boy who was just too heavy. I denied and denied. Then I started to panic. Then I went straight to Google.

Immediately, juice was banned. No juice. Not even diluted. He reacted to this new rule not unlike a possessed child being splashed with holy water. He writhed. He screamed. I think I actually saw his head rotate 360 degrees. But the no-juice rule stayed.

But the chub was still there.

I was put on my first diet at the age of eleven. This involved turning up to group meetings with grown women in a church hall, slipping off my shoes and being publicly weighed.

I was counting kilojoules and whipping skim milk into fluff, as a snack, before I had left primary school. I didn't want anything like this for my son. But in my desire to avoid the demonisation of food and the low self-esteem it inevitably creates, I had unwittingly set my beautiful son on a rocky path.

It wasn't until I took him to his first day of creche that I saw how different he was. The other kids seemed so small compared with my little sweetheart, whose shoes and pants were at least two sizes bigger. Mild panic set in. What happens if someone is mean to him? What happens when, after three years of being told he is magnificent, someone tells him otherwise, based on his weight? I could barely breathe.

Last month, he had his check-up with the maternal health nurse, and that was when the news of his extra seven kilos was broken. The nurse was wonderful about it, and I'm certain it's not an easy conversation to have. Mercifully, my concern was palpable. She knew I was out of my depth and gently suggested I go to see a paediatric dietitian.

This sent me into a spiral. For as long as I can remember, eating disorders and an obsession with weight have been a girls-only domain. Girls I knew in the '80s were eating only a packet of chicken-noodle soup and a green apple for the entire day. And they were thirteen. I was one of them. Sadly, statistics show that boys are not immune to this madness.

I imagined turning up to a clinical office, my baby being stripped and weighed.

I imagined this as the day his self-loathing would be born. I called the dietitian and asked if it was necessary for her to sight my son, as I was paranoid about him being made to feel that he was anything less than perfect. She assured me it was necessary to see him, but it would be okay.

I knew she would ask me what a typical day of food entailed for him and I thought she would think I was lying. But this is a child who doesn't know chicken nuggets. He's never had a fish finger. He hates cream. Sure, he loses his mind and acts like a kelpie off a leash at a party with cake, but don't all kids?

I told her what he eats. Fruit. Lots of fruit. Cheese. Toast. Chicken breast. No other meat. He will eat around the meat in a spaghetti bolognaise, which is quite a skill. She listened intently for twenty minutes while I expressed my bafflement. Then she helped me.

My three-year-old eats too much good stuff. Turns out that four bananas a day, if you're only one metre tall, will make you fat. And if you throw in three mandarins, a punnet of strawberries and four Cheestiks, you're in a pair of size-6 elasticised jeans before you can say, "Is it creche today?"

My shame for getting him into this mess has turned to relief. He's now eating all the things he knows and loves, just far less of them ... and not every day!

But we are the lucky ones. We can afford to see a professional who will probably change our lives. We are also a family who know about good food, grow vegetables and always have a bowl of fruit on the table (or up high in the pantry now, to stop the daily disappearance of five kiwi fruit). What happens to the kids whose families have no idea about nutrition, and no money to talk to someone about it? I am an educated woman with a wealth of knowledge about food, and even I stuffed up badly. It's all very well to bleat on about the obesity epidemic, but until we make education about basic nutrition accessible for everyone, it will just get worse.

3rd June 2012

A very adult toy story

My magazine editor casually mentioned to me over email that the next issue's cover story would be about vibrators and sex toys and if I could just explore that topic a bit ... it might be nice ... a little tie-in. I quickly tapped out an email saying that I couldn't possibly write about that as I found the whole concept to be a bit "icky". That's the exact word I used. Icky.

Then I thought, why do I find it, as I so intellectually put it, icky? What's wrong with it? And if every woman is harbouring a plastic gherkin with an on/off switch in her knickers drawer, then why can't I?

I went to a Catholic girls' school. Now, before you jump to any conclusions about me wandering the timber halls protecting my candle from the breeze during prayer vigils (and let's be honest, there was a fair bit of that), let me just say for the record that if I could've had a boyfriend, I would've. I had rampaging crushes that inspired behaviour that today would probably get me jailed for stalking. I obsessed. I calculated compatibility according to how many letters our combined names had in common with the word "loves". If I got a low score with the boy I was in love with I'd just change the spelling. I tried this trick with everyone I ever met, and only stopped when

42

I'd reached a rare 99 per cent compatibility with Omar Camel.[1]

Boys were just a mystery. I never knew what to say when they were talking to me. I felt like the guys I knew wanted small, quiet blonde girls. Not big, brunette, curly ones who belly-laughed and loved the Smiths. I always felt so conspicuous, and "less" than.

I clearly remember watching a film clip in 1986, possibly on *Countdown.* The song was "Breakout" by a one-hit-wonder band called Swing Out Sister. They had a bob-haired woman as the singer and two other male members. I studied the clip intently, and learnt all the words.

That achieved, I continued on with thoughts such as: "Wow. That woman is in a band with men. They're not married ... so they must be friends? Imagine having a male friend? What do they talk about? Is she always trying to keep quiet and not be funny? Do they want to kiss her even though she looks like a bit of a show-off?"

So I never had any boyfriends and was deeply jealous of the girl at our school who was rumoured to be "doing it". Boohoo.

But now I believe I've hit the man jackpot. My fella is both charming and sexy. He really likes me, and I like him, and we are enormously happy, and, frankly,

---

[1] Omar was a camel ride at the local fair.

I don't want to mess with it by doing what many articles suggest and go off to "buy a vibrator together". I just can't imagine it. I would laugh. A lot. Then I'd get worried it would get weird and I'd have to mumble, "Only joking. Let's get home to the kids." Oh, yeah. Foxy. That's me!

I've even heard people say that women who are adamant they don't have a toy at home are lying. I assure you, I'm not lying.

It may be a generational thing. Those "aids", in my memory, are sold in creepy stores that always seem to be accessible only via a shady doorway and a flight of stairs. The windows are painted out. If anything, I've always found this particular line of merchandise to be funny, not sexy. And definitely just for other people.

It seems, though, that women have been secreting away these pleasure machines for decades. My friend's brother actually found a little something in his own mum's shelves. Let's say he got a little more than he bargained for one Sunday afternoon in the '80s while playing murder in the dark in her walk-in wardrobe. Technically, he wasn't snooping ... because who knew glow-in-the-dark technology and sex toys were a match made in heaven? The horror/hilarity of this story has gone down in folklore among that group of friends. And his mother's name, Brenda, is now only pronounced "Brrrrrrrrrrrrrrenda".

Perhaps that has scarred me? The hushed laughter we all shared over that story has meant that this topic has hitherto meant comedy, not titillation. There's no doubt, as I write this, that I am showing my age, conservatism and possibly immaturity.

But by all accounts "things have changed" ... so excuse me while I get enlightened and turn to the naughty pages in the magazine. I always did love a sealed section!

10th June 2012

Cold-weather warmers

There is a lot to dislike about winter. It's cold, for a start. And I, for one, always seem to be in a maniacal hurry from one form of heating (car, office, home) to another and back again. My skin cracks up from the change in climate. My winter coat gets snugger year on year. And I don't like scarves. But all these negatives magically disappear when you remember that there is soup. And shanks. And mash.

Nothing puts me in a better mood than when I stop at my local butcher to pick up some chicken bones for my world-famous cream of chicken soup. Meticulously dicing the celery and carrot is not just a recipe step ... I kind of commune with them.

Summer in Australia is the stuff of legend. November hits and the suburbs are awash, or at least mine is, with the smoky aroma of sizzling snags and fatty lamb chops. But let's not forget the chillier cousin. Winter is the season when the oven comes into its own. And it's also the season when I happily pull out all my nifty appliances that have been gathering dust while the metal skewers and salad servers get a good workout. I have a slow cooker. I think I wept when I chose the one with a timer. This means I can throw all sorts of things in it before I go to work, and when I get home the smell of succulent chicken pieces, herbs from the garden and sweet, translucent shallots greets me before my three-year-old has even had a chance to tear around the corner on his trike.

Nothing says, "Welcome home," like the smell of a winter meal.

I remember playing in the streets around my house when I was about six years old. We lived in a newish suburb in the late '70s and there were lots of dark-brown brick and quarry tiles and ferneries. There were also great casseroles. Early one evening, in that delicious free time between primary school knock-off and when Dad wanted to watch the news, I was playing with an Indian boy who lived close to my place. We might have been having a heated discussion about which Kiss member we most identified with and – bang! – it hit us: the aromatic waft of a slow-cooked-from-scratch curry.

Kavin's mother was a petite woman who wore bright saris and said very little. I believe that when you know your way around a cumin seed and a knob of ghee like she did, you can let your cooking do the talking. Instead of calling out to her children to come in for dinner, or ringing a bell (as my Irish Catholic friend's mother used to do), she would simply open the front door of her home. Slowly, the warm smells of dinner would creep out into the street and tell Kavin he was about to get the feed of his life.

Discussion stopped. He ran inside. And I moseyed back to my place for my evening meal, probably of apricot chicken. Or, if it was *Blankety Blanks* night, Rice-a-Riso.

The cooler months are the patron saints of home. We can't wait to get back there. In summer we're always out. We're splashing in pools, picnicking in parks and licking ice-creams on bustling streets at 8pm, because we can. Not in winter. Winter is for corduroy and remote controls. For mugs of things and doonas. For lamb shoulder and pork belly.

In fact, I think roasts might just be the overall heroes of winter. I was always scared of roasting a chook and only perfected my technique a few years ago. A crisp-skinned bird, stuffed with rosemary, parsley and thyme and a lemon, if I have one, is to me the perfect frosty weather treat. It ticks all the boxes. Delicious, obviously. Economical, yes (there's the next-day sangas, stock from the bones and let's not forget the sneaky post-dinner clean-up "pickover"). But there's also the chicken smell. It's a smell that says to my family that I love them madly. It fills the house and even surrounds the garden with the misty aroma of care. Even the next-door neighbours can smell it. I like to think they get envious.

And when my fella has been out all day working on a building site, hunched over a tepid sausage roll for smoko, then listening to the dire traffic reports on the radio on the way home, it makes me swell with pride knowing that as soon as he pulls into our driveway, he will take great sniffs of a home-cooked meal. The house will be warm. He will come in, dump his little blue lunchbox, unzip his coat and say, "Dinner smells great, Cakie." For me, that means job done.

Now ... why am I so hungry?

17th June 2012

Clowning around for a good cause

My parents thought they had finished having their children in their twenties, just as all their friends had. So when, in her thirties, Mum discovered she was pregnant with me, she was, to put it mildly, surprised. My sisters were much older than me and all our family friends had children of similar age, so I spent my childhood really feeling like the odd one out.

It never crossed my mind that someone's mum could be pregnant because I'd never seen it. At primary school my friends' mothers must have finished their families, too, because no one ever welcomed a baby sister or brother. We all dreamt about it, but it never happened – until Year 5 when a schoolmate announced her mum was having a baby.

I eyed her mother off at school pick-up and watched her belly grow. I was two parts fascinated and one part jealous as hell. Wasn't it every ten-year-old girl's dream to have a real live baby at home to put in a stroller and dress up like Holly Hobbie?

At the last school pick-up of the year, I saw my friend's mum in something smocky, heaving her other small kids into the Nissan Prairie, and I knew that by the time we'd covered our maths books in contact paper for the following year, she'd be strapping another little one into the people mover.

But that was not to be. When we returned to school there was no baby.

He had been born. He had been named. He had been shuttled home in a hand-me-down baby suit to the embraces of his eager siblings and awe-struck parents. But one morning, a few weeks into his new life, he did not wake up. He just didn't. No symptoms, no illness, no warning. He was gone.

And that was my first experience with the unfathomable horror that is sudden infant death syndrome (SIDS). I can imagine nothing knocks you down quite so quickly and permanently as losing a baby.

When my babies were small (and not so small) I would get such a thrill walking into their bedrooms to see them first thing in the morning. To find your baby still and silent when you excitedly go to see their face ... well. Even the thought of it brings tears to my eyes and a little crack across my heart.

A few years after my friend lost her baby brother, Red Nose Day – run by the SIDS and Kids charity – began. Initially, I thought the idea was crass. It was such a serious thing, to lose a baby. How can we clown around about it? But as Red Nose Day became so popular, so visible, so effective, I realised the red nose was not about making light of a devastating topic – it was about making a point. It was about speaking about the unspeakable.

Red Nose Day has worked. The research that has been done by SIDS and Kids has been, quite literally, life-saving. The fact that we sleep our babies on their backs, keep their cots uncluttered, keep them in the same room as us where possible and breastfeed if we can is reducing cases of sudden infant death syndrome every single day.

We weren't always doing all of that before. Plenty of families have cringeworthy recollections, usually with a '60s or '70s soundtrack, of their mother, her mouth with a ciggie hanging out of it, rearranging a toy-infested bassinet and wondering, "If a nightie is highly inflammable, does it mean it's likely or unlikely to go up in flames when placed in front of a molten-lava bar heater?"

We have come so, so far.

Since the first Red Nose Day was held in 1988, cases of infant death by SIDS have decreased by 80 per cent. That's thousands of babies who are now growing up and destroying rusks and writing notes to Santa and dragging their parents to *Dora the Explorer Live!* Thousands. Of. Babies.

We can thank SIDS and Kids for this, but we can thank ourselves, too. By buying that silly red nose and putting it on our faces, or on the front of our car or our office building, we have contributed to life-saving research.

I always buy whatever I can from the SIDS and Kids card table outside my supermarket, and when my children were newborn I popped onto their website to make sure I was doing everything I could to reduce the risks.

So if you can spare a few dollars on the next Red Nose Day, I can just see the thousands of tiny hands that will applaud you – or high-five you, if you're into that instead.

24th June 2012

Self-appointed experts

I ask for advice all the time. My main sounding board is my fella, The Chippie, who gives great, no-nonsense and harshly concise advice that often contains an expletive. I like it that way, because more often than not in the lead-up to actually asking for said advice I've spent countless hours umming and aahing and writing lists of pros and cons. By the time I get around to asking his opinion I'm usually so confused I need a verbal smackdown.

For example, when I was making a huge decision to leave a job for another I endured most of the indecisive torment on my own. Until I'd come to an impasse. I broached the topic with The Chippie and here's how it went:

"So ... what should I do?"

"You like hanging out with your kids. Take a job that makes that happen. And if it doesn't work out, then do something else. I'm going to the shed."

And so the decision was made.

I seek counsel on matters of couches, throws and shrugs from my friend Jane. She's earned her stripes through her passionate hatred of orange. Anyone who feels so strongly about a colour must know all there is to know about interiors. She also multi-tasks as an adviser on parenting – her daughter is spirited, polite and artistic and maybe I want one just like that.

I am constantly asking for advice and eagerly await responses from my crack team of clever friends. But what about advice that is given when you didn't ask for it? Has this ever happened to you?

This week I have received no fewer than three pieces of unsolicited advice and, as a result, I have experienced unprecedented levels of huffiness. First, a no-brainer. Someone emailed me with advice on weight loss. It didn't have the subject "Lose that jelly belly NOW!" – I have a spam filter for those. It was from, I think, a nutrition student and probably made a lot of sense, had I read it all. But I didn't ask for help or advice from this person and it annoyed me. It doesn't take a genius to know I am overweight but is it anyone's right to assume I need advice on the matter, or indeed that I want to change or am not already seeking advice elsewhere?

The next day I received an email from someone instructing me on the dos and don'ts of writing a column. I thank you, by the way, and I hope I'm doing an all-right job. I love writing these pieces but I am under no illusion that I am the next Proust. I have in the past solicited advice from people I admire, but the difference is I asked for it. The notes in the email I received were handy. But insulting. As I was reading it, all I could hear was my internal dialogue saying, "Clearly I'm bad at this and I didn't even know it."

Which brings me to the last bit of unsolicited advice I got in my inbox. This one happened yesterday. And it involved the P word. Parenting – there is no more sensitive topic. The person who sent the email thought I'd be "interested in attending a parenting workshop". Hold up? As a participant? Yes: as someone who wasn't "enjoying their children as much as they should" and could work on being a "confident and calm" parent.

It's not often I talk to my iPad. Apart from the occasional "Yes!" after nabbing a set of old school lockers or a *Toy Story 3* Zurg figurine on eBay, our relationship is generally a mute one. But on this occasion I looked at its screen, cosy in a case my mother-in-law gave me for my birthday, and said, "Oh. My. God."

Parenting workshops are a great idea and provide support and ideas for people who need them. FOR PEOPLE WHO NEED THEM. I'm not saying I'm a perfect parent but how you raise your kids, along with every other thing you do in your life, is up to you. If we identify parts of our lives that are causing us concern, then we have the right to seek advice. What is crucial, though, is that we come to identify our problems and shortcomings ourselves, not have them brought to light by people who are making bold assumptions based on, well, nothing at all.

We can almost cope with unsolicited advice from people within our lives but when it comes from those you've never met, who've never seen your home/what you eat/how you cope with your kids in the midst of a supermarket meltdown, then "helpful pointers" are not only ridiculous, they're hurtful. And only fuel the insecurities that threaten to slow us down when we're all just doing the best we can.

1st July 2012

Super 8 memories

I have known my partner for just over five years. In that time we have had two children, signed on for a crippling mortgage, built a gigantic deck, installed a remote on our fifty-year-old garage door and located all the local pubs where "kids eat free". As you can tell, all the important stuff has been achieved with great speed or, as my dad says, "You don't muck around, do you, darling?"

One of my life's regrets (apart from not being born Greek ... the gyros, the plate smashing, the abundance of family, dancing and spits over the barbecue in the backyard) is that I met my partner when he was thirty-two years old and not when he was one day old.

Weirdly, we grew up within about four kilometres of each other, he with his brothers, and me with my sisters. I think we even spent our pocket money on lay-bys at the same toy store called Griselda's. Great times.

Luckily, his father made movies. Lots of them. In the early '70s, he invested in a Super 8 camera. No doubt, it would have been a massive outlay because, from what I can gather, back in the day blocks of land were sold for $5 a square foot, and TVs were roughly $4 million. Sure, seems fair. Anyway, my father-in-law set about documenting every baptism, birthday, picnic and backyard burn-off that occurred in that family from about 1972 to 1983. The eight-millimetre film was then left in a box for twenty-five years or so until about two weeks ago, when my partner, The Chippie (aka the second-born son), took them all away and had them converted to DVD.

What happened next was one of the most memorable days of my life. Because I pressed play and there he was: as a baby, as a boy. The man I knew better than anyone, in a time before "we" even existed. His first birthday party, in 1976, was held in a garden shed, the table piled with Iced VoVos, home-made chocolate cake and bright-orange cocktail frankfurts. The chubby blond baby in the metal and orange vinyl high chair looked bewildered by the fuss. His Uncle George, resplendent in Barry Gibb-style chest hair and an open-neck terry-towel tee, tenderly ran a hand over the birthday babe's round little head in a gesture of such familiarity and love that it caught in my throat.

The films are achingly sweet – and hilarious. Outside a cathedral on the occasion of one son's baptism, the lens swiftly veers from a cavalcade of safari-suited parishioners to an unfolding drama in which a Hillman Hunter is in flames in the middle of the road. Reminded of the scene, The Chippie's dad exclaimed, "That's right! A car exploded!"

I'm a naturally nostalgic person, so these home movies, hours of them, are my idea of heaven. In their flickering frames, I saw faces that confirmed with one look the kind, memorable people I'd only been told about. The Chippie's paternal grandmother passed away decades before I came on the scene and I'd heard wonderful things about her. Gentle, they said. And sweet. And funny. And what a cook! To see her, fussing in the kitchen and cheekily shooing away the Super 8 with a tea towel, or sitting quietly on the couch as the family socialised around her, confirmed without words the kind of woman she was. I felt I'd met her.

The Chippie's family knew how to live large. Weekends were about charred snags on makeshift barbecues, kung-fu fighting under the Hills Hoist or driving the Torana to a sunny spot to feast on egg sandwiches and Auntie Norma's world-famous cakes. They got out and about en masse. Not to theme parks or shopping centres or the movies. Just being together was the event. It's inspiring.

My favourite scene is in the lounge room of the old house where The Chippie grew up with his parents, brothers and his blue-collar, happy-faced Grandfather Popsy. Popsy was a mountain of a man who raised his daughters, one of whom is my mother-in-law, after their mother was taken suddenly by breast cancer. I'd heard he had a big heart. Now I could see it. Because there he was, silently, on my TV, shiny with joy, in his impossibly crowded lounge room, dancing what looked to be the dance of *Zorba the Greek.* These, I thought, are clearly my kind of people.

I believe in fate. Perhaps my yearning to have been born Greek is a nod to my children's great-grandfather, who, despite having been born Irish Catholic, could summon an internal bouzouki with the best of them.

8th July 2012

Reverse bucket list

Everyone is making bucket lists. A bucket list, in case you haven't heard, is a list of things you want to achieve before you kick the bucket. Common activities on this list include skydiving, riding the Orient Express and learning to cha-cha. You get the drift.

I have always found the term obnoxious, like when people put their hand up and say, "Too much information." It just sticks in my craw. Or maybe it touches my immortality nerve. I haven't bought life insurance, either – because, like my "cousin" Bella Swan from *Twilight,* I plan on living forever.

Instead, I'm putting together a reverse bucket list of the things I'm not going to do before I perform my final shuffle. This seems so much easier to achieve. So, here we go:

I will never...

1. Learn to make pasta. I've attempted this and my kitchen ends up looking as if the marshmallow man from *Ghostbusters* has left leprous parts of himself all over my benchtop. The pasta turns out to be a crossbreed between Clag and rubber bands. San Remo will do me fine, thank you.

2. Jump from anywhere high (attached to a parachute or a perky other person). This has zero appeal. People say it makes them feel alive. You

know what makes me feel alive? A strong coffee. On my own. In a cafe courtyard. No emergency straps required. Which brings me neatly to...

3. Order skim milk. Takeaway coffee is wildly overpriced, and yet I buy it. Indeed, I worship it. Why would I pay good money for sugary, blueish milk when I can get the good stuff? I can tell when a barista has mistakenly used skim in my double-shot flat white by looking at the bubbles. They look like detergent. And taste like it, too. Pass.

4. Be horrified when my children swear. I wish I could be better at this. But I just can't. Every time my three-year-old drops the Sh-bomb, I have to bury my face in the cupboard so he can't see that I think he's funnier than Tina Fey. Bad Mummy.

5. Grow anything resembling vegetables in my patch. No matter how I try, my parsnips look like chicken bones, my rocket is positively Jurassic, and my zucchinis could give Dirk Diggler a run for his money.

6. Align the number of books I buy with the number of books I can physically read. I've done a little maths, and if I were to read all the books I own, I'd be horizontal for 243 years. Fine for Nosferatu. But I have to work.

7. See the pyramids. Why?

8. Climb a tree. See above.

9. Read *Fifty Shades of Grey.* Controversial, I know, but I have no interest. I was sitting on a plane next to a woman who, with a sneaky smile, ripped her copy out as soon as the spiel about the oxygen masks was over. I read two lines over her shoulder, and the woman gave me a dirty look as if I was the creepiest person around. Hey! Take it easy. I'm not the one with a thought bubble over my head with a throbbing gland in it, lady. Sheesh.

10. Buy a sports car. I'll never get this. I love station wagons because they're practical. Fast cars can be as fast as they like but the speed limit is the speed limit and no matter how much car you have, you still have to stick to sixty. It's like attending a luau: there may be a whole suckling pig but your stomach can only take so much. My friend, who has a car roughly the size of a nit, did a big supermarket shop at Christmas and had to call me so I could take some bags home for her. That's right. In my station wagon.

11. Get a Brazilian (again). Devotees of this brutal, humiliating procedure insist it's the best thing since Stevia, but I tried it once and I had to book in for therapy. The beautician told me, while my leg was over her shoulder, that her

oldest client was seventy-seven – which adds a whole new disturbing vibe to *The Golden Girls.*

12. Skin a kangaroo tail. That's right. Skin a kangaroo tail. My friend, who works with indigenous communities in the NT, wanted to do something special for her friends. She googled a recipe and off she went. Step one: skin tail. These tails are roughly the size of a pool noodle, but covered in hide. When I left her, she was steaming each fur-covered pool noodle and peeling it millimetre by millimetre. She was in a sweaty frenzy, and muttering, "Maybe there was a reason they traditionally throw these in the fire first." I didn't have the heart to mention that big groups of people are usually happy with lasagne.

15th July 2012

Unmarried and proud

What is your marital status? It seems like such an easy question to answer. But it isn't. I have two small children and a giant mortgage and a wonderful partner to whom I am totally committed. But I am not married.

I always squirm at the question because I'm not married, but the other option is "single" and, Lord knows, I ain't that, either.

The fact that I have never tied the knot hasn't been due to a philosophical stance. Unlike Brad and Angelina, I've never said I'm waiting for marriage equality before heading down the aisle to a Shania Twain song. I kind of just never got around to it. Well, why not?

We've all seen the TV wedding shows and lost count of the number of scenes in which, eyes wet with tears, a woman with newly visible collarbones looks down the lens and says, "This is the day I've been dreaming of my whole life."

I was never one of those. As a child, I never dreamt of a wedding. I was mad about having babies and nursed kittens, dolls and, more alarmingly, a wheat bag in a bonnet.

But I never played dress-ups in my mother's wedding frock. In my imaginative games, even Barbie and Ken were living in sin. I don't think I was an early feminist; marriage just never struck me as a milestone.

My Barbie was always more focused on remodelling her living room and providing for Skipper, who was her little sister, personal assistant and foster child on a rotating roster. Sometimes Ken was gay. And everyone knows gay men can't get married (well, not in Australia).

Don't get me wrong, I love weddings. I am always the first to weep at the vows. It is such a beautiful, raw moment when, in front of everyone the bride and groom hold dear, each says they love that one person the most of all. I tear up just thinking about it.

So why haven't I done it?

I was "with child" about a year into my relationship with my fella. The simple answer is, we just didn't make it a priority and then – boom – we were having a baby, and getting married felt like asking someone who had just eaten an entire Black Forest gateau if they'd like a slice of cake. Redundant.

There is also the small issue of my very shy partner. His idea of fresh hell is to be looked at, even adoringly, by hundreds of loved ones. To add a cake-cutting photo opportunity and a slow waltz to Aerosmith's "I Don't Want to Miss a Thing" to this scenario would bring on months of counselling.

I've never been officially asked, either. I'm old-fashioned in that I'd feel weird getting down on one knee and asking a man to marry me. I have no problem being the breadwinner. But marriage? I think it'd be up to the fella.

And then maybe also I've never been thin enough. Giant white frocks are the natural enemy of size-22 women, of which I am one. I remember hearing Dawn French, the curvy comedian, talk about her wedding in the '80s to funny fellow Lenny Henry. She starved herself down to a size 10, got hitched, then had to do it all again a couple of years later so she'd recognise the woman in the photos.

So now here we are. Five years down the track with my bloke. Totally committed, two gorgeous children, a beautiful blended army of mutual friends.

My dad has stopped asking me when we're going to get married. A traditionalist, it took him some time to get his head around the fact that his daughter was living in sin, but when he saw how my man could hang a door and change a nappy, he knew he'd got a bona fide son-in-law – even without the papers to prove it.

I'm organising a Christmas-in-July party for tonight. Thirty-five of our nearest and dearest buddies are going to indulge in amazing French food at my favourite restaurant. Parlour games will not be out of the question, and someone will probably dress up as a wonky Santa and give out stupid presents.

A few of my friends have asked, "Is this one of those secret weddings?" and I admit I did think about popping into the registry office, making it official, then celebrating the certificate with all our friends. My partner has always said he wants to get married but doesn't want the wedding. I'm not mad on a registry-office affair. I think I'd be wanting to register my car, too, in a two-for-one deal.

So it leaves us happily together with no papers. And in the end, I suppose, if it ain't broke, don't fix it.

22nd July 2012

Crafty plans

I once met the amazing Pip Lincolne from Melbourne. She is a master craftslady, has written three beautiful crafty books and drinks cups of tea behind the counter of her amazing shop full of cute bespoke bits and pieces. She has sparkly blue eyes and a blunt black bob and she wears cardigans and has a son called Remy. She's one of those people you meet and within a few minutes you're thinking, "I would not mind at all if I wake up tomorrow and I AM Pip Lincolne."

This happened to me when I did a TV segment with her in which we made cushions out of old shirts and greeting cards out of op-shop copies of Golden Books. After being in her orbit for just a few short minutes, I had tantalising visions of me making little pencil cases at home in my craft room with a cat on my lap and Carole King on my iPod. I would wear a wooden owl brooch and eat home-made plum cake and drink Lady Grey tea from a polka dot cup. I would be the Queen of Pencil Cases! I'd have a pencil case for every occasion!

All I needed, Pip said, was a sewing machine. Which reminded me, I did have a crack at sewing once when I was in my early twenties and literally sewed through my finger. Twice. I actually had to unpick the stitch out of my index finger with a Quick Unpick.

In primary school I was a dab hand at finger knitting. Who needs actual needles when you have fingers? I made several holey, long, skinny sheaths of wool using only my index fingers. Their purpose is still a great mystery to me.

My grandmother was amazing at crochet. She was a woman possessed, really. She'd spend the lion's share of her pension on hand towels, face washers and tea towels from Best & Less and proceed to trim each of them with crochet. Every time I'd visit her she'd make me sit in front of her chair as she plucked each work of art from a bag, laid it across her lap, and met my gaze expectantly, waiting for a unique reaction for each one.

I ran out of adjectives after the 113th facecloth. When she passed away she left me her timber cribbage board in the shape of Australia and all her crochet patterns. She must have picked me as a fellow craftslady.

So, inspired by Gran and Pip Lincolne and those "Here's How To" pages in the paper, I decided I really needed a sewing machine.

I rallied my sisters and best friend and begged for a Husqvarna for my birthday. Thrilled at the suggestion (apparently I'm hard to buy for and, strangely, none of them had thought of a sewing machine as a possible gift ... wonder why?), they dutifully purchased it and wrapped it up, and I clapped when they presented it to me over strawberry melbas and coffee.

I'd had it for a whole week and hadn't opened the box. Then a month passed.

Then a couple of months. Then I had another birthday. Then I had another baby. Then I did my kitchen. Then I started a new job.

Life was certainly busy, but every so often I'd make sure to find a few moments to indulge in a pang of guilt and mourn the loss of my crafty dream.

I now realise it's not going to happen. I'm just not that person. I don't like Lady Grey. I prefer Joni Mitchell to Carole King. I don't have a craft room. Or a cat who likes to sit. Sadly, the sewing machine is staying in its box. It's going to be two years in November.

I might even put it on eBay.

Actually, maybe I could exchange it for a pasta machine! I'm sure they do that sort of thing on Gumtree. I have this vision of making all my own pasta ... from scratch.

I can see it as clear as day! I'll spend whole weekends scooping big handfuls of semolina out of a fabric sack and wiping my floury hands on my red checked apron ... a village dog will be milling around my glazed terracotta floor collecting scraps and I'll clap and say, "Prego!" then crack fresh eggs with one hand.

Or maybe I'll just go to the local and buy a packet of spaghetti. And a pencil case.

29th July 2012

Obeying your gut feeling

I've been sick. Very sick. This week, I met gastro face to face. And even though I liked it about as much as I like a person who brings out a calculator to divvy up a dinner bill, I am kind of grateful it visited because, weirdly, I learnt some stuff about myself.

I was talking to my friend Mel about the dreaded lurgy. We had our babies a few weeks apart a year ago. She had a long and spine-chilling labour. She gives a softly spoken warning before she tells anyone about it because if it was a movie, it would be classified by adult themes, horror and obscene language. And even Mel said, "Proper gastro is like childbirth. It makes you crazy. If someone offered you a choice between death, or living through it, there's a chance, in your rank stupor, that you could quite easily take the former." She has a point.

Being out of action when you have small children is terrible. I was holed up in my bedroom, acting like whatever that was that lived under the stairs in *The Munsters.* I was drifting in and out of consciousness, snatching small conversations with my three-year-old, who would tentatively enter the room, climb on the bed and engage in conversations like:

"Mummy ... are you okay?"

"Not really, no. I have a bug."

"Is it a ... ladybug?"

Then he'd scuttle away and I'd hear him saying in an adult voice to his dad, "I don't think Mummy's going to make it."

I wanted to assure him I would, but I was out of it again, flattened like a wounded seahorse, in my nest of towels. Remind me to burn those, okay?

My one-year-old, we decided, was not to be touched by me at all. I knew I might be contagious and wanted desperately for this little angel to be spared twenty-four hours of acting like something from *The Exorcist.* So he would come in in his dad's arms, catch sight of me, then be whisked away *Sophie's Choice* style, screaming with arms outstretched. I would mutter something like, "Trust me, kid, this is not the mummy you want today." But it was terrible. Just terrible. The great news is that after approximately forty dry heaves and feeling like I'd done three days of ab crunches, it passed. Just like that. And I could enjoy Saladas for fun, not survival.

My family is my kingdom. I spend every waking hour making sure they have a beautiful, kind, comfortable and enriching life. It is my life. It is ours. I am present in it every minute of every day. It is my very favourite thing to do. My very favourite place to be. So it is very odd to be absent. To step down. I found it a bit confronting. I don't think I'm a control freak.

I just felt like I was missing out on something. Meals were prepared. Eaten. Baths taken. Hair washed. Stories read. Even Buzz Lightyear crises were averted. In the distance, down the hallway at lunchtime, I heard the fridge open and in my head I was screaming, "There's a chicken, sweet potato and chia stew I made for baby Kit in resealable tubs!" But, as in a bad dream, nothing came out.

The world, to my surprise, did not end.

I am not a sickie-taker, either, but I took TWO whole mornings off my brekky radio show. I warned my boss with a text message at 11pm. It was simply a photo of my current view: the toilet bowl and the words, "Something evil this way comes." At 2am I texted again, this time from over the kitchen sink, and said I didn't think my 4.30am alarm would be obeyed. Not this morning. Or the morning after, as it turned out.

But guess what? The radio show went to air. It was great. The world didn't end.

It is refreshing to find that, despite my belief to the contrary, I am not the centre of the universe. Despite the well-thumbed and scribbled-upon pages of my old-fashioned paper diary, I can put a big fat red cross through two or three whole days and nothing diabolical happens. One rogue microbe, lodged in my gut, taught me that it's okay to let go occasionally and that people will cope.

Thank you, gastro, for letting me give the incredible people around me a bit more credit for their roles as oarsmen in the canoe of our life. Because sometimes that bossy one who rides along the shore on her bike screaming into a megaphone can hit a rock and come a cropper. And guess what? The canoe will still slide through the water just as it always has. Thank you, gastro. Thank you.

5th August 2012

Gym evasion

I'm being stalked. My tormenter is not clad in a sci-fi merchandise T-shirt, sporting a greasy comb-over, nor is he at my window clocking intimate moments such as me defrosting the mince for dinner or hooking rogue mandarin pips from the mouth of my crawler. No. He is stalking me by phone. From his gym.

I've been a member of four gyms in my life. The first time I signed up and literally never set foot in there again. That "free" assessment ended up costing me more than $1000 and a fair nudge to my self-esteem. The other times I just lost interest because treadmills were boring. But that was then.

This time, I'm enjoying it. I am forking out for a personal trainer, which should be a tax deduction because, Lord knows, the people who really need the help can't afford it. Me included. But it's the only way for me. I'm treating it like piano tuition. I'll stick with the trainer until I have the vaguest idea of what the hell I'm supposed to be doing, then I'll be confident to continue on my own.

I've committed to a half-hour session three times a week, and while I'm still waiting to get that endorphin rush everyone tells me will make me addicted, I love that I'm doing something for my body and making it strong and capable. It's quite fun.

Finding the time is an issue at the moment, though. I've just started filming for a weekly show, which takes a day out of my week. Poof. Gone. I have a normal job, too, and, these two elements, along with a feverish pull to get home to roll around with my kids as soon as possible every day, means I need a gym that will be a bit understanding.

People who work at gyms must have heard every excuse for non-attendance in the book. Most of them, I admit, have been uttered by yours truly at one time or another. In the '90s, I told one place I was sick, then never contacted them again, hoping they would think I was dead. Didn't work.

'90s gym girl: "Hi, Chrissie! It's been seventeen days since we've heard from you! Are you dead? Ha ha."

'90s me: "Yes. Makes crunches difficult."

What is it about breaking a gym membership that turns us all into liars? If it were anything else, we'd just say we can't do it any more. So why do we act all crazy?

I think it's because we know we're going to be judged. And no one wants to be called lazy or, even worse, have it be true. So we lie. And act strange. I feel for the gym staff, having to communicate with us when we're acting as if we're a mere three signatures away from being committed.

Yes, I've tried every tactic. But guess what, new gym guy? I'm not foxing this time!

I want to be in your establishment. I like your cross-trainer. I appreciate that lifting stuff until my face quivers is good for me and I'm enjoying it. But I'm busy. It's the truth this time. Is that so hard to believe? Apparently so.

I received a text message from my gym guy yesterday. He hadn't heard from me in five days and he was getting worried. (I'd been flattened by gastro.) It was a picture message. Well-meaning harassment just got creative!

He had seen a billboard with my face on it spruiking the fact that I'm on breakfast radio. This thing is massive. He'd artfully positioned his camera to make sure his head was next to mine. The resulting photo was my giant, beaming face next to his faux-angry one. Accompanying the pic were the words, "It's time for Chrissie & Gym Guy time. Monday!"

I laughed. Then I realised that no matter what I said, he would hear, "Blah, blah, lie."

I started to compose a text message, which was, of course, lies, despite the fact the reasons for my temporary disappearance were legitimate. I immediately went into the kind of panicky avoidance you indulge in when you're in the supermarket looking like hell and buying tampons and you spy the mean girl from school. Avoid! Act dodgy!

Then I called him. And I told him the truth. I told him I love his gym. I love the half an hour I put aside to make my body stronger. I told him I'd been stymied by illness and a change to my workload. I said I'd be back next week.

He was quiet for a minute. The truth? He almost didn't know how to handle it. And I almost didn't know how to tell it. I felt so empowered. And I promised him I would not be calling him in six months to tell him I'd contracted something, moved interstate or had, in fact, passed away. How grown up.

12th August 2012

Uncomplicated men

I haven't lived a life full of men. In fact, quite the opposite. I am the youngest of three sisters and my parents separated when I was five. Dad moved to Adelaide while we all stayed in Melbourne. We had four boy cousins, but they all lived in Queensland. Or Canberra. Or somewhere. Add to that the fact I went to all-girls' schools from Year 3 onwards and you could be forgiven for thinking that my life was loosely modelled on Louisa May Alcott's *Little Women.* I even have a sister called Beth.

For the first twenty years of my life, men were a great mystery to me. Growing up, I never knew how I was supposed to act around them. I got all my cues from movies and TV. Greg Brady, Darrin Stephens and Pa Ingalls all added pieces to the jigsaw puzzle of what men meant to me. I gathered this info and concluded that men like flares, crazy paving and slopping up stew with cornbread after a hard day's woodchoppin'.

I met my first true love when I was studying teaching. I followed him to his pigeonhole and learnt his name was Lee. Later that month, I ran into him by chance in the city and we sat in a greasy spoon and fed coins into the little jukebox. We bonded over our mutual appreciation of Massive Attack and Madonna. We stayed together through share houses, graduations, internships and jobs. We had two fights in seven years. The first was over whether or not Ginger Spice was sexy and the second was over whether or not he should go on a tacky bucks' night at a strip joint. He went. And got decked. That was the end of his foray into sleaziness.

I've been lucky in that I haven't had too much exposure to the men your friends have warned you about. I just haven't met them. Or if I have, I haven't let them into my world. I'm sure they exist ... but not in my universe.

When I worked in advertising I met dozens of creative, hilarious gentlemen. They never wanted to sleep with me, so I was free to love them with complete fervour. I caught up with one fellow eight years after he first gave me my chance at a career in advertising and I thanked him. He told me he never hired anyone he wouldn't like to sleep with.

We guffawed over this. And I was flattered. Not horrified. There haven't been too many men in my life who have hit on me, and frankly I'll take attention wherever it comes!

I've always appreciated a man's uncomplicated nature. All the women I know are also as transparent. It's a trait I like.

People say that men are from Mars and women are from Venus, and I probably would have agreed with that statement in my teens. The boys on my tram, smelling of a curious "boy blend" of pencil shavings, hockey sticks, orange rind and cheap deodorant, were the most intimidating people I'd ever seen. I'd stare at their school bags just to see what was inside. I was fact-finding. Like Miss Marple, but with newly shaved legs and navy hair ribbon.

But as I've grown, mainly into myself, I can't muster one example of a man I do not understand. The one I live with now is a dream. Funny, honest and hard-working – like all the women in my life. And I have two little boys of my own and five nephews (no nieces), so now I'm swimming in boys. They are all I know. My sisters and I are trying to raise these tiny human beings to be empathetic, kind and industrious. Just as we would if they wore tutus instead of tool belts. They are defined by their lack of drama. They are a good influence on us all.

When I was twenty-nine, I was thrown into the *Big Brother* house and it was there I learnt the most about men. I remember thinking at the time, "They're so fun!"

Men have taught me to not sweat the small stuff. They run at life without considering the drama of it all, the consequences. Life is a trip.

Last night, in a sea of toys and kids' stuff, with four baskets of washing to fold and a 4am wake-up looming, I was attempting to get my one-year-old into a romper suit for bed. It was like trying to get an octopus into a plastic bag. Sensing my panic, my partner looked at me with his shiny eyes, scruffy beard and a wry grin and said, "Marriage, kids ... the whole catastrophe, eh?"

How do they do that? With one sentence I was able to let it all go and enjoy the chaos.

Men. Maybe it's true, you can't live without them. And why would you want to?

19th August 2012

We can meet heroes

Rick Springfield was in Australia. My friend Tim sent me a link to an article that stated the "Jessie's Girl" singer had done an impromptu show at a suburban restaurant. One surprised diner said, "I was having lunch with a couple of friends, then the band changed and a few older blokes sang three songs. It wasn't until he was singing 'Jessie's Girl' that we realised one of them was, in fact, Rick Springfield."

This is deeply un-Australian. I would have lost my tiny mind. In fact, if I was enjoying a parma at the Cove Steakhouse and Rick goddamn Springfield turned up, someone would probably have had to call triple 0.

I can't tell you exactly why I love him so much. It could be his dreaminess, but it's probably the fact he wrote these genius lyrics: "I wanna tell her that I love her, but the point is probably moot."

I don't live too far from the restaurant in question, so I could've staked out the place. But I've recently learnt that you have to be careful when you meet your hero. Tread carefully. Very carefully.

You see, my first love was Simon Le Bon from Duran Duran. My sisters and I dreamed of the band every night. When they toured Australia in the early '80s, my sisters even saved their pennies and caught a TAA flight to Sydney to stalk them. Our sorority owns every vinyl album they have ever released, even *Night Versions* – essentially laborious 45-minute versions of the radio edits we loved on *Countdown.* We were hardcore. And it's a love that has not waned.

So you can imagine my boundless joy when, earlier this year, I was given an opportunity to interview the band, then meet them backstage before their stadium show. When I told my sister she'd better organise a babysitter as she was finally going to see them face to face, she cried. We both did.

First came the interview. I sat down with two members, John Taylor and Roger Taylor. I bored them senseless. I told them how much they meant to me. They had no interest whatsoever. Then I tried to get all cerebral and ask serious questions about their influences, but I'd lost them at hello. Within two minutes, they had lost the will to live. When I'm nervous and humiliated, my voice goes high and tight, as if I'm choking on sourdough, so all the interview yielded was a few minutes of me asking inane questions. I couldn't even listen to the edited audio. Such shame.

This didn't bode well for the meet-and-greet planned for later that night. I didn't tell my sister of my horror. Instead, I cleared the bread from my throat and soldiered on.

We met outside the arena squealing. We had lipstick on and fully charged iPhones.

My sister warned me that I was about to see a side of her I might not like. "I'm going to be kind of gross and excited, you know?" I told her it was okay. I'd love her anyway. We were ushered backstage, where we waited. And waited.

Eventually, we were corralled into a long hallway and asked to wait against the wall, firing-squad-style. There was a kerfuffle and then they appeared, all five members, including the lead singer, Simon Le Bon. A few other fans carried bits and pieces to have signed, but my sister and I just wanted the photo. Finally. A photo. After thirty years of admiration, we wanted three minutes of their time ... and they treated us like something they'd stepped in during an outdoor Pilates class. Then it was over. They walked on stage; we went to our seats. We couldn't even look at each other, the humiliation was so great.

It took us a few weeks to admit how horrible it was. How bad we felt about ourselves and the disappointment that our fandom was misguided. It is hard for your feelings not to be hurt when your idols make you feel stupid for liking them.

As I said, you have to be careful what you wish for. I'd heard that meeting someone you greatly admire often ends in tears and now I've learnt about it firsthand.

So, Rick Springfield, if it's all the same to you, I'll hide my love for you under a bushel. I'll keep the feelings of adoration pure. And I'll be watching you with my eyeeeesss and I'll be lovin' you with my body, you just know it ... and I'll be holdin' you in my arms late, late at night...

Because it's probably better to keep some mystery about what it'd be like to be Jessie's Girl than to find out for sure.

26th August 2012

Crap dates and motorbike loans

I was recently visiting my newfound love, the online bookstore, and something caught my eye just as I was about to hand over my credit-card details. Admittedly, I do know them off by heart, so there is not a lot of time between punching in the numbers, hitting confirm and high-fiving myself for organising the speedy (and free!) delivery of yet another selection of books I do not have the time to read.

But there it was, causing a rare pause in my Pavlovian book-purchase response – a hardcover called *Crap Dates.* Just like the Summer Roll impulse buy at the checkout, I knew this baby had to be mine. And so it was.

A few days later, it arrived and I found myself stirring my chicken soup while chuckling over succinct recollections of the worst dates in history. Succinct because they come from an idea from Twitter to convey the most appalling date stories in history in just 140 characters. Irresistible. Here's what I would have contributed. (All names have been changed to protect the unhinged.)

He thought saying he killed a robber with his own boot would impress me. So I agreed to another date because my friends begged me.

I'd met Kade through a friend and he seemed okay. A bit ruddy and greasy-looking, which I liked at the time because it indicated he had a fondness for wine, and in my late twenties this was as important as an ability to breathe. He was kind of annoying but his compulsive lying was so entertaining and I had no one else on the radar, so I saw him three or four times. Dates would start at a restaurant and usually end up at my place so he could lie to me uninterrupted while I frantically tried to remember all the ridiculous things he'd say. My friends would religiously call me the next morning for a debrief.

The lies were fairly standard: he was the adopted son of the Ansell condom king; he was dropped on their doorstep with a $10 note attached to his romper suit. You know, Fibs 101. He had also been an SAS soldier, which came in really handy, as it turned out, when he had to pin down a robber at his local milk bar with his army-issue boot until the thief expired. I'm sure it would have been spooky if it wasn't so darn HILARIOUS.

What he didn't count on, though, was that I was really listening. He mentioned the milk bar where this heinous (and strangely unreported crime) was committed and, to his horror, I knew the place. I get my milk and Helga's from Dave, the owner, every day. "What are the odds!?" I said. "I'll bring it up next time I see him!"

At this, Pinocchio got twitchy. He quickly suggested I shouldn't mention it because it was so traumatic that Dave's memory would have deleted any recollection of it for his own good. Really, Kade? Or here's another theory, Kade. Maybe Dave wouldn't recall the fact that someone had died in front of his mixed-lollies cabinet from a boot to the throat because, I don't know ... it didn't happen.

That was the last time I saw him, much to my friends' great sadness. The best news about this "relationship" ending, though, was that it put the next one into perspective.

Knowing I was vegetarian, he took me to a meat-pie shop. But not before visiting a bank to apply for a loan for a motorbike. While I waited.

This one was a ripper! Jimmy looked like Tim Finn, a look I'd long admired. He had a nervous habit of twirling his curly fringe into something resembling the hair that plumbers have to extract in one long piece from shower drainpipes. He picked me up and said he just had to pop in to the bank. "Score!" I thought. "We're not going Dutch!" I waited, fixing my hair and readjusting the pale-blue Wayfarer knock-offs I'd bought from Target.

After an hour, I started to empathise with those dogs you sometimes see tied to trolley barriers while their owners do the supermarket shopping. Will he ever come back? Why are all these people patting my head? Where is my water bowl?

After ninety full minutes, he returned to the car thrilled to the back teeth because he'd been approved for a motorbike loan. By that stage, I was too busy snapping at my itchy bits like a flea-ridden dog to care.

It's easy to pass these off as what they undeniably are: crap dates. They stink of disrespect and deceit. But are bad dates a waste of time? Not at all. I'd go on them all again (and, dear reader, there are MANY more stories where these come from). They're funny. I love that the world is full of people not like me. And sometimes we have them in our living room and, yes, even in our bed.

My gran always used to say, "Every pot has its lid," and it's true. And as pots, we have to enjoy trying on as many lids as we can, even if sometimes they're square and we're round, or we're teapots and they're, well ... crackpots. I have no doubt that both Kade and Jimmy have found the loves of their lives now. Though I suspect Jimmy may have to register his one true love with the council.

2nd September 2012

"Having it all"

I've been doing a few interviews lately because I've started a new job as the host of *Can of Worms.* It's the usual roster of radio and press commitments and, frankly, the usual roster of questions. The first one I am asked, without exception, is: "How does it feel to have it all?" Of course, what the journos and broadcasters are referring to is the fact that I have two small children and I hold down a breakfast-radio job as well as the once-a-week hosting duties for the TV show.

I'm not sure why, but every time I'm asked that question I have the overwhelming desire to poke someone in the eye. Because what is the answer? Am I supposed to take a swig of Krug and bleat, "Graysh, thanks! It feels ahmahzing to have it all, thanks so much for noticing." The fact is, though, that from the inside, from where I stand, "having it all" just feels kind of like having a job and having kids. Nothing more and nothing less.

I read a great quote this week: "The reason we struggle with insecurity is we compare our behind-the-scenes with every one's highlight reel."

Well, to answer the question, "How does it feel to have it all?" I offer the following insights into my own behind-the-scenes …

1. My alarm goes off at 4.45am. I sneak out of the marital bed and get dressed in the kitchen because everyone is still asleep. I lay my clothes out the night before and sometimes forget my shoes or undergarments, so at least once a week I turn up to the studio with no shoes/a floppy maternity bra/no undies.

2. I could probably get up a bit earlier and run a straightener over my hair, but I opt for the extra fifteen minutes of sleep. The drawback of this is that I spend the majority of my day looking like an escapee from an asylum.

3. I always forget to make sure there are enough bananas. We run out of them – often. And they're the only fruit my one-year-old will eat.

4. Last week, I put my three-year-old to bed and quickly read him a story. I confess I skipped every second page and invented The End when I felt like it.

5. Weet-Bix and blueberries can double as dinner.

6. I just measured a hair on my leg and it came in at an impressive 1.2 centimetres. Clearly, I need a Post-it note in the bathroom that says "shave".

7. Last week, my gas was nearly cut off because I forgot to pay the bill. I had to call them and beg for an extension, spurred on by visions of my children in layers of clothing huddled around the cat for warmth.

8. I made a terrible waldorf salad and chicken spare ribs for dinner and I couldn't even talk about how foul it was. Later that night, I heard my partner stirring up a glass of Fybogel to make up for the distinct lack of edible anything in the meal department.

9. The "service me NOW" light has been on in my car for about four months – but, seriously, how can I survive without the car for two days? I will probably drive it until it explodes. And work it out then.

10. My three-year-old knows fifteen types of dinosaur and I have no idea who taught him. Where have I been?

So there you have it. That's what "having it all" feels like. If it sounds familiar, that's because it is. It's life. It is what living feels like. It's busy and disappointing and being spread too thin. It's also joyful and crazy and rewarding and funny. It's the same as your life. Every time I read an article on women "having it all", it is accompanied by a picture of a model in a crisp black suit, looking exasperated and juggling a smart phone and a teddy bear. What a load of rubbish.

Actually, maybe I just found that elusive thing that deserves that poke in the eye?

9th September 2012

Too much information

Yesterday I laughed so hard I sprayed coffee out of my nose. In truth, this sort of thing happens to me often because I rate having a guffaw very highly on my daily to-do list – along with breathing, nuzzling my sons in that area between their shoulder and neck and singing Adele songs loudly. All good things.

I also really love it when something embarrassing happens to me. It gives me a thrill. Even as the humiliating event is unfolding, with me at the centre of it, I am at the very same time delighting in the thought of the imminent retelling of the excruciating details of the story to an appreciative audience of friends/sisters/colleagues. When you have a group of likeminded people to enjoy your mortification, everything is funny.

Last week I stopped by a cut-price department store to pick up some baby onesies and some undies. I was mooching around with my three-year-old in the trolley when a tiny woman approached me in the baby department and breathed a whispery warning in my ear. "You have a hole in your pantssss," she said. Then immediately she vanished. Not unlike Snape from *Harry Potter.* Or Slugworth, the creepy guy who approaches each golden ticket winner in *Charlie and the Chocolate Factory.*

I immediately reached my hand around to feel for the hole and all I felt was bottom. A hole indeed. I tried to pull down my jumper to cover my exposed rump. When that failed I thought, "Imagine you don't know your bum is hanging out and finish your shopping with a cheeky nonchalance."

And so I did. Albeit with apologetic eyes to anyone who had the misfortune of waiting behind me at the cash registers.

When I told my friend this story, she screamed and threw herself back in her chair. We laughed breathlessly for ten minutes straight. Delightful.

And it seems I'm not alone in my compulsion to share embarrassing stories.

The next day on my radio show, we opened the phone lines on mortifying moments and Kay called in with a cracker that left us speechless.

She had been to the dentist and had a tooth removed. One of the back ones, the ones that leave you open to the glamorous affliction called "dry socket". Hot.

Anyway, Kay had the procedure and was feeling pretty fine, actually. Not one to waste a day off from work, she decided on a spot of retail therapy at her local shopping centre. You know, sashay through some shops, grab a muffin ... ordinary stuff made exhilarating by getting to do it during work hours on an unexpected day off. It's heaven, actually.

So Kay parked her car and checked her appearance: looking good, given something the size of a stock cube had been extracted from the bones of her face just an hour earlier. Feeling brave, she removed the wad of gauze, locked the car and off she went.

About an hour later, and after browsing several thousand racks of discounted pastel jeans, she blew her nose and saw a spot of blood on the tissue. Problem.

She made her way to the conveniences and within seconds realised something had gone seriously wrong with the whole stock-cube extraction situation. The lower part of her face was covered in blood. She'd been walking the shopping centre aisles, asking "Do you have this in a size 12?" and "What's the muffin of the day?" with a face that resembled something from a documentary about lions, impalas and feeding frenzies.

When she told us this story she could barely get it out. And my on-air partner Jane and I had moments of not even being able to hear what she was saying because we were howling like malamutes.

Some people call this "oversharing" but to me there's no such thing. If Kay and I are telling stories that make some people put up the palms and squeal "Too much information!" then so be it. Even Rodney, who followed Kay on air, was not guilty of oversharing by my standards ... even though his embarrassing moment involved the car park at a place called

Tropical Fruit World, a funny tummy and mincing back to the car with his wife yelling after him, "Rodney! I can see something! What have you DONE?"

And in the interests of those who are vehemently anti-overshare, I'll leave it there.

Enjoy your coffee.

16th September 2012

Grand illusions

We have decided to pull up stumps and move closer to the city. We live in a suburb that was settled in the '60s ... all big blocks and fir trees and optimistic architecture.

And we've loved it. The peace, the quiet, the parking! But I suddenly got the notion that I wanted to be somewhere that smelled like garlic from restaurant kitchens on Friday nights, so we're off.

The house has, of course, never looked better. After four years of turning my key in a chipped mission-brown front door, it is now a glossy fire-engine red. The door I always wanted. We removed approximately five tonnes of weeds and nameless shrubs from the front yard and planted neat hedges and feature plants. It's beautiful. The garage is like something from a TV series. In fact, the whole house is dreamy. Why exactly are we moving?

Let me tell you, it is no mean feat taking a house from Octomom to Martha Stewart. Especially when I am a naturally messy person and I have two little fellas under age three to contend with. The solution? Hire a storage unit. One day, when my three-year-old, Leo, was at kindergarten, two removalists came and took away a truckload of our life clutter. Leo's room looks like no child has ever even breathed in there. Every so often he'll get a faraway look in his eye and

I know it's coming … I know he's remembering his old room and the questions are about to roll.

He'll say, "Where's my cubby house?" or "Where's my train table?" To which I mumble something about aspirational buyers and selling the dream. He'll get his stuff back eventually, but right now it's important that his room resembles a still from a kids' manchester catalogue. I may or may not have manufactured a twee "reading station" with colour-coded books and a Pippi Longstocking-themed rug. The devil, or the profit, as my real estate agent tells me, is in the details.

On "open for inspection" days, I fly around the house like interiors queen Tonia Todman on speed. A bowl of lemons appears on the coffee table. I usually have to artfully turn a few around to hide the bite marks, because my toddler finds them irresistible. I scream nonsensical things like, "Those apples are not for eating, they're for SHOW!" and "Why is there still a sticker on that Packham pear?"

The en suite, usually the domain of a left-out hairdryer, charging toothbrushes and my fella's beard clippers, is now host to a solitary Oriental lily in full bloom, a green Venetian candle and a pump of Aesop handwash.

Hopefully, the prospective buyers never need to wash their hands, because what they'll find lurking in the fancy bottle is actually a cut-price refill.

I even have stunt towels. Bright white and never used, they are artfully placed on the rails ten minutes before the buyers arrive because, hey, doesn't every family have pure white towels?

Then there are the pillows. Nothing sells a house like 4000 pillows. I have them on the main bed, the living-room sofa, every easychair and even in the cot.

In my baby's bedroom, the poo bin is stashed away. No one wants to see evidence of an actual human baby. Lord knows they're not going to find any of that at our place. I am ashamed to admit that there is a chair in the baby's room, complete with cushion and small side table with three thoughtfully fanned out Beatrix Potter books. I have never sat in the chair, I have never opened those books. Hell, I've never even read *Jemima*

Puddle-Duck to my one-year-old! But let's not let the truth get in the way of a good story, shall we?

And you know what? It's working. People love the house. They're eating it up. But I suspect what they're really falling for is not the bricks and mortar. It's the irrational belief that if they buy this house, they'll be the sort of person who has fresh tulips in the dunny.

They're buying being the family who always makes the beds and has a kitchen that is 90 per cent shiny benchtops and bowls of perfectly formed navel oranges. They see themselves entertaining their friends in the "alfresco barbecue terrace" and their excitement ignores that fact that it is just a patch of Lilydale Topping with a ten-year-old Super A-Mart table on it and a $10 blooming cyclamen in a terracotta pot.

Part of me wants to stop them on the way in and say, "It's all a dream! We don't live like this! NO ONE LIVES LIKE THIS!" But that would be beside the point.

I have been tempted, however, to include in the contract a small disclaimer along the lines of: "Purchasing this house does not include children who live like Little Lord Fauntleroy. Your husband will still leave chest hair on the soap, wet towels on the floor and abominable odours in the WC. And the indoor grill is a bastard to clean. You will use it once and stick to the frying pan."

Let's see what happens come auction day...

23rd September 2012

Learning to lie

My child has learnt to lie and it is both worrying and delightful to me. I guess you have to be careful what you wish for, because when he was about six months and I was getting impatient to converse with him, I remember saying to my partner, "I can't wait until he can talk! And, you know, start fibbing."

I've always loved watching tiny people concoct whopping great lies. Mainly because they have no idea how obvious it is that they're lying. When you know, you can enjoy the performance.

Last week we noticed our above-ground pool (better than a beach in your own backyard!) had started to develop a slowly dwindling water level. If the slightest thing goes wrong with it I call the professionals immediately. Frankly, it's like a big blue moody mistress is living in my garden: great times to be had, but you don't want to hear about its problems. Within a few days, someone in a wetsuit had found a hole and patched it and we were all fine.

It was on this pool guy that my three-year-old decided to unleash his very first lie. Leo loves a visitor, even a tradie. He follows them around, chatting and inspecting their work. First stop with any pool problems is the filter-and-engine thingy. In our case, the machinery is housed under the decking in a dirty, spider-infested crawlspace. I've never been in there because it gives me the creeps, but pool guys and three-year-olds are clearly impervious to its perils and in they both went. It was a beautiful day so I was standing outside holding my one-year-old and listening to the barrage of questions that Leo was firing at the pool guy: "Is that a spanner?" "Is that your tool bag?" "Did you know my dad sometimes locks me in here?"

Ummm ... what?

That's right. My son was telling a total stranger that sometimes, you know, just for kicks, his dad LOCKS HIM UNDER THE DECK WITH THE POOL MACHINERY.

Before anyone calls the authorities, I can assure you that I have spent many hours with both the accused and the alleged victim, and Leo's dad has a hard time keeping a straight face even while telling him off for breaking his favourite Star Wars figurine.

I mentioned the Pool Guy Incident to my friend and she said, "Yep. He's nearly four. That's when they start lying like rugs. It's hilarious. But also scary. Caitlyn told everyone at kindy I had a hairy penis."

Another friend confessed she'd been called to the school because her daughter told her teacher that Mummy had chopped up her bed and stopped giving her breakfast.

I must confess, I remember the first whopper I ever told. It was 1979 and I was playing at the Penrys' house at the end of the street. For some unknown reason, when Mrs Penry asked how I was, I feigned sadness and told her my dad had died ... in the war.

Maybe I'd been watching too much *Apocalypse Now,* who knows? The strangest thing is that now, as an adult, I have no idea why those adults believed me. Sure, there was a war going on between Vietnam and China, and the Cold War was yet to wind down, but 1979 wasn't a big year for Australian involvement in wars of any kind. And besides, they'd probably slowed down the Falcon and had a quick chat to Dad while he was mowing the lawn that very weekend. Why didn't they know I was lying?

Nevertheless, Mrs Penry turned up on our doorstep with a CorningWare pot full of curried sausages and a message of condolence. I came to the door behind Mum just at the moment Mrs Penry was mouthing something mournful to her. The penny dropped as I realised what the curried snags meant. My immediate reaction was to bundle my things into a handkerchief, attach them to a stick and hit the road forever, hobo-style.

But I had to face the music. Thank goodness my mother was sensible and realised I was four years old and just, well, lying my bottom off. I'm not sure Dad was even told about it. It might have hurt his feelings, actually...

Perhaps it's tales like these that prompted the story I heard recently about a local primary school slipping notes in the schoolbags of its pupils, cutting a deal with parents: "If you don't believe most of what your child says about school, we won't believe most of what they say about what goes on at home."

Deal? Deal!

30th September 2012

A comeback for all insults

There are some things you should never say to a woman. You know what I mean: sometimes things are said to you that strip the oxygen from your lungs.

The annoying part of such an unexpected assault is that you very rarely have a quip at the ready. Your arsenal of smartness is almost always empty. And you drive home or walk away shell-shocked, only to spend the next few hours coming up with the most brilliantly crafted and scathing retorts. Why do we NEVER get the chance to say these to the actual people who've insulted us? Damn them!

There's a great TV program called *The Catherine Tate Show.* In it, Tate plays several characters and one of them is an androgynous man called Derek who everyone assumes is gay. But every time someone says something that infers that, he exclaims in horror, "How very DARE you!"

It's something that my friends and I have worked into our everyday language. Here are some great ways to use it (and yes, all these exchanges really happened):

A woman went to see her obstetrician as she was expecting her second child. She was maybe a size 16. And thirty-six weeks pregnant. In the room were the doctor and a student nurse. The doctor asked if she'd been using the services of a specialist pregnancy dietitian and she replied no, that she'd used one for her last pregnancy and was using the skills she'd learnt during that time. The doctor looked wryly at the nurse and said, "Looks like she ate him."

"HOW. VERY. DARE. YOU!"

Fiona and her husband had been through a rough year. He'd been diagnosed with a terrible illness and things were not looking good. Six months after the grave diagnosis, a "friend" sidled up to Fiona at a barbecue and said in a hushed voice, "You might want to try to lose a little bit of weight, because when your husband dies you're going to have trouble finding a new one." (This actually happened.)

"HOW. VERY. DARE. YOU!"

My friend Jane was coming home with her first baby – a magnificent baby girl. Her next-door neighbour met her at the gate and asked excitedly, "What did you have?" Proudly, Jane replied, "A girl!" To which her neighbour replied, "Oh. Doesn't matter. Next time you'll get a boy."

"HOW. VERY. DARE. YOU!"

About five years ago, I was sitting with my back to the office door. I was deep in concentration reading something. I didn't even notice my colleague come in the door, so I didn't lift my head. The first indication I had that I wasn't alone was an index finger poking me in the back and then under my arm and a familiar voice saying, "Back fat! Back fat! Side boob! Side boob!"

All right, it's true that both of those things exist on my ample body ... but do you really have to poke them?

"HOW. VERY. DARE. YOU!"

A friend was getting a spray tan – now, I've never done this, but I imagine you feel pretty vulnerable when you're nude, apart from a paper G-string, in front of a total stranger.

My friend is not even vaguely overweight, yet the spray tanner started off by asking her to "lift your saggy boobs". Great. Step two was to offer some extra service. "I'm going to help you out," she said, "and give you some definition on your tummy where you have none." And for the finale: "Arms up! Let's not forget those bingo wings!"

Two things. Firstly, my friend will find somewhere else to get both her tan and her insults. And secondly...

"HOW. VERY. DARE. YOU!"

So there you have it. The ultimate weapon when someone says something unbelievable to you. It's my gift to you, and it will let you deal with the offence immediately, instead of mulling over it for days and muttering the ultimate comeback under your breath to no one but yourself. You're welcome.

7th October 2012

The kindness of strangers

Something happened last month that restored my faith in the human race. In fact, it happened twice. Someone, a complete stranger, changed my tyre for me without having to be asked.

The first time, I'd taken off on a short trip to get milk. Leo was with me in the car because, Lord knows, even popping up to the servo to get some milk is an adventure when you're three. After a few minutes I noticed a hideous burning rubber smell.

Now, I'm no mechanic, but even I know that when a car smells like burning rubber it's not a good sign. When I followed my nose to the source of the odour I saw my tyre was flat, down to the rim, and about 4000 degrees in temperature.

I had absolutely no idea what to do. I was stuck with a pre-schooler, a molten-lava wheel and lapsed (of course) membership to one of those roadside-assistance thingies. When I'm in a situation that I can't see a way out of, I get hot and sort of huffy. And I'm not afraid to tell you that by now I was hot as hell and huffing like a Biggest Loser.

Enter Paul: kitchen designer by day, anonymous wheel-changing superhero by, er, day as well. He waltzed over to my car, asked where my spare was and got to work.

I was flabbergasted to see that lurking under a secret trapdoor in my boot was an emergency tyre. And all this time I thought my boot was a mobile storage facility for kid-size hard-hats, dried-out packets of baby wipes, half-gnawed rusks and a stroller I've used twice. Who knew!

If you've never seen someone changing a wheel (as I hadn't), imagine yourself with a stranger who is writhing around on the ground in a fashion not dissimilar to those wildlife warriors who try to tag crocodiles. Those tyres sure do put up a fight, by the looks of things. But Paul got me all sorted out. He even called his mate at the local tyre shop, so when I arrived there they knew what sort of tyre I needed and I was fixed up and on my way in no time.

I was actually teary when I thanked Paul for his kindness. It was the kindest thing anyone had ever done for me.

Until a week later, when I was turning into an eight-lane freeway and I heard a bang. My first instinct was to check my head for a bullet hole (don't you worry, I've seen *Underbelly*). My second was to utter under my breath, "Not another tyre!"

So there I was, stranded again for the second time in a week with a flat tyre and no idea. I should have paid attention to Paul, but I seriously didn't think I'd need to so quickly.

However, within five minutes a handsome fellow with a ten-year-old son had pulled over, taken my keys and was reversing my wonky vehicle into the service road. Again, I pushed aside the rubbish in my boot to reveal the by-now well-worn emergency wheel and he set about changing it for me.

This time he made me work for it a little bit, and I had to loosen a nut. This involved me bending over, bottom in the air, whispering "Righty tighty, lefty loosey" at the rims so I'd get the direction right. Eventually, the wheel was changed and I was on my way. I looked at the handsome man's son and said, "Your dad is a hero, you realise?" He just shrugged and went back to playing his Nintendo DS.

What struck me about the kindness of these two gentlemen was that they absolutely did not have to help me. They both had things they were doing and could have easily just stuck to their schedules. I've done that. Plenty of times. I've seen someone in a broken-down car looking frantic and I've thought, "Well ... what can I do?"

Now I'm paying it forward. I paid a lot of attention when the handsome stranger was changing my tyre and, having also done a crash course on YouTube, I'm confident I can now change a tyre without creating a dangerous situation à la *Wacky Races.*

And next time I see a woman with a flat tyre, gesticulating wildly while on the phone to someone,

I'm going to pull over and change her wheel. I bet it'll feel really good.

14th October 2012

Raising boys

I think I'm onto myself. Yep, the jig is up, as my gran used to say. I have, I believe, taken the easy way to parenthood by being a mother to boys and not girls. In fact, I think that if I ever have a third child and it is a girl, I will fully lose my mind.

I wonder if other mothers of boys are thinking the same thing I am.

I have friends with little girls. I feel like they know I don't really know what I'm doing in the parenting stakes. And I'm talking about the kids, not their parents. Little girls just seem to have my number. They are all-knowing. They are serious and smart and switched on. They seem to know I have no idea.

I was eavesdropping on a conversation the other day between my six-year-old god-daughter and her grandpa. The lovely old fellow was talking to her about party food and how if she ate too much she'd get a tummy ache. She fixed him with a withering stare and said, "Don't patronise me, Grandpa." Boom!

I have two sons and sometimes I think this is God's way of acknowledging that, as a parent and as a person, I mean well but am generally too goofy to be trusted with a proper responsibility.

Raising a daughter seems so ... complicated. It scares me. How could I possibly navigate the scary minefields of self-esteem and eating disorders so prevalent in the lives of girls? How could I ever live with the guilt if I got it all wrong?

I have a very clear idea about the kind of men I'd like to raise. I'm raising them to be kind and respectful, with a healthy appreciation of fun and manners. So far, so good. And I suppose raising a daughter would be the same in some respects.

So why am I so spooked? Are they really that different to boys? They seem so much more sophisticated, even from an early age. Little girls seem more powerful, more formidable. Bringing up a daughter feels to me like a greater responsibility somehow.

I just feel like I'd be getting away with less.

My friend was telling me the other day that her daughter gave her a mini-counselling session in the car. After the ten-year-old had stopped singing all the words to the new Bruno Mars song, she turned to her mother and suggested she take better care of her appearance and maybe tried wearing a few "younger" things, because it was obvious she was a beautiful woman but she wasn't, and I quote, "doing herself any favours". Ten years old. And she wasn't being disrespectful. My friend was wide-eyed over her latte when she whispered to me, "Know what the spookiest thing is? She's RIGHT!"

How could her daughter, who has only been alive since 2002, know so much? And how would I deal with a daughter of my own, looking at me with my own eyes, telling me truths I knew but didn't want to, or simply could not, admit? That's what I'm scared of.

Girls are strong – the ones I know seem to have been born with a great idea of who they are and it's up to the parents to figure it out. I'm just nervous that I'll misjudge them. That I'll think they're an A when really they're a B. Tears, slamming doors and the words "I hate you" will ensue.

My sons are so straightforward. And I have found parenting them so darned easy. A joy. Lots of cuddles, lots of laughs, lots of running around, lots of stories and away you go. Girls just seem like the real deal to me. Emotional, thoughtful, analytical. Argh!

I will have to keep my fingers crossed that if a girl ever does come along into our goofy old lives I won't totally lose the plot and take my parenting cues from *Ab Fab*'s Eddy Monsoon or *The Lohan Guide to Raising Girls*.

21st October 2012

Letters to your younger self

There's a craze that's gone bonkers, and, no, I'm not talking about the hyper-charismatic Korean genius who goes by the name of Psy and has taught preschoolers and grandparents alike to stroke their own legs while singing, "Heeeyyyy, sexy lady!"

I'm talking about the trend of writing letters to your ten-year-old self. The letters started dripping in a few years ago and, since then, they've become a deluge of pretty much the same warnings. The most common of these include, "don't let the turkeys get you down", "you will find someone who really loves you" and "don't believe that mean girl when she tells you you're fat and useless".

When I turned ten, something extraordinary happened. My mum gave me my own key to the family home so I could let myself in after school and I never looked back. In fact, it was a great year. I wore shoes from Sportsgirl and listened to Wham!'s *Make It Big* and saved up all my pocket money for a cat which ended up celebrating my twenty-seventh birthday with me. Things were sweet. And, frankly, if I could go back to 1984, all I'd say to myself is, "You probably do need a bra for those sore little walnut boozies but, apart from that, carry on."

Not so to my 23-year-old self. So let's go instead to 1996...

Dear Chrissie,

Are your eyes feeling small and toxic because you ate four home-brand dim sims last night for dinner? Thought so. That's cool. One day you'll be able to afford something exotic like rocket and bocconcini, so don't sweat it. I do, however, wish to point out that if you hadn't just sunk yourself into debt for that white Grundig TV, you'd probably be enjoying a plate of something nutritious right now. But choices are what define us and, in truth, TV is going to be important. So get another bag of dimmies.

I think it's great that you've enrolled in your dream university course to finally chase your goal of becoming an advertising copywriter. It took a lot of effort and you were right to celebrate it with 14,000 bottles of lambrusco and all your naughty friends. Remember to recycle those bottles as candle holders, by the way. You'll need them in a few years when you host share-house board-game nights attended by friends and four families of mice.

About uni, I should bring to your attention that you will need to actually attend some tutorials, and by this I don't mean sitting in a city cafe, smoking with your hairy mate Nick Swifte, drinking coffee and plotting whose notes you'll scam. Also, when the other people in your course see you in a lecture and exclaim, "What?! Chrissie's here? There must be a test!" this is not a compliment.

Let's go now to the beauty department. You're all right. No real problems ... but that matte lipstick makes you look like you sleep in a coffin. It also comes off in sheets on those coffee cups you're so fond of studying during "tutorials". Give it up. And wax your upper lip. Do it now and you will avoid an embarrassing intervention in a few years from your gay housemate.

Your boyfriend is a great fellow, and when you finally break up with him after seven years you will think it was a waste of time because it didn't end in a ring and babies. Don't. That relationship was a lovely safe house through your whole twenties and meant you avoided most of the types of men you'll meet in your thirties. And anyway, if you had married that guy and had kids you wouldn't have the man and little boys you have now and they are awesome and worth waiting for.

Finally, you are terrible with money right now and are focused on fun over almost anything else. Accept it. You are not going to change. You are in big trouble from your mum right now for buying that apple-green vase for $95. True, this amount represents a week's rent and half a month's payment plan on the parking fine debt you've accrued for leaving your Daihatsu Charade wherever the hell you like for however long you want.

Tell your mum to back off. That vase will bring you joy your whole life and give you a thrill every time you look at it because it represents that you had faith that one day you'd be able to afford a few beautiful things and have a lovely house with gorgeous people in it that you made.

And so it will be.

Warmest regards,

Chrissie (at one week from thirty-nine years old)

PS I mean it about the moustache. And for God's sake don't bleach it. Just because it's orange doesn't mean it's invisible.

28th October 2012

Naughty schoolgirl

I was recently contacted by my old high school and I was delighted. For many people, their school years were fraught with a combo of not fitting in, bullying and bad papier-mâché puppets. I'm pleased to say only the latter applied to me. I went to a small private Catholic girls' school, which is a sentence that usually ends in "and I couldn't wait to escape" or "and they were the worst years of my life", but I loved school.

I was one of those kids who couldn't wait for school holidays to be over, and I got so worked up the day before we went back I usually had instant-onset insomnia. One time I was so excited that I found myself having a shower at three in the morning so I wouldn't miss my 7.20am tram.

So the phone call from the school alerting me to the fact I'd been nominated as an "alumni of note" was met with excitement and internal clapping, not horror and avoidance.

Part of this honour was that I would be featured in a coffee-table book showcasing the 125 years the school had successfully educated girls in the ways of needlepoint and hymn-singing, human rights and Shakespeare.

It was, and still is, a lovely school that turns out smart, independent women year after year. A few that come to mind are the brilliant comedians Jane Turner and Marg Downey, as well as High Court judges and innovative doctors. Apparently you can rub shoulders with these luminaries if you make a living talking about boozies, babies and big bottoms ... but who am I to object?

I was invited to come to "the parlour", a room at the school that was strictly out of bounds to anyone in brown T-bar shoes and ponytails. I was met by two photographers, who told me they wanted me to take them to a spot in the school that held memories for me.

So, first things first, I asked to be taken to the huge Chesterfield sofas that were parked at reception, where the naughty girls had to spend their lunchtimes. But the Chesterfields had gone. No problem ... what about a shot of me at the careers counsellor's office? This was where I was told one afternoon that my test results had come in and I was most suited to a life spent in the circus. Nope. Those offices were now home to whirring servers.

Hmm ... I know! Why don't we go into the chapel, where, in one corner, much to the delight of me and my teenaged friends, we discovered a life-size plaster version of Jesus's head? Sadly, that was gone, too.

We tried several different locations, but all to no avail. The secret air vent where we would sneak up to whisper demonic messages to the bewildered class below was shut off. The timber box built to house an air conditioner, but which doubled as an excellent place for fourteen breathless seventeen-year-olds to cram in and hide, had been removed. The Year 12 common room that we had eventually been banned from for too much smoking and a rat infestation had become a tasteful breakout area for what I imagine are much better-behaved girls than we ever were.

Eventually, I settled for a shot in front of the wall on which we used to play handball when we were nine years old. One of the only memories I had of school, apparently, that didn't involve breaking the rules!

"You were pretty naughty," the photographer said as location after location fell flat. I'd always thought I was a good student. I had a ball at school, but I had no idea I was so damned badly behaved. No wonder I didn't get the marks I needed for law! I was clearly too busy plotting mischief and thinking of new ways to crack up my friends. Shame on me.

But maybe this is the sign of a truly remarkable school – I never felt like the bad kid. I was never defined by my naughtiness. Perhaps those nuns and teachers recognised that sometimes kids like me needed to be allowed to be a bit of a larrikin in order to survive in the world.

I hope that my school, and others like it, aren't extinguishing the fires in feisty girls these days. Because being a buttoned-down lawyer or commodities trader is well and good and lucrative, sure, but sometimes girls are better suited to a life behind the mic, or in front of a camera sporting lycra and a tight blonde perm saying, "Look at moyyy." Or indeed, as my careers counsellor suggested, pursuing a life under the Big Top. Follow your bliss, girls, no matter how long you have to spend on that squeaky Chesterfield.

4th November 2012

The M-word

Misogyny is the buzzword of the moment and it seems everything and anything from politicians to entire cultures are being accused of it, while new articles every week blow the cover of one industry or another and the lady-haters who work within them.

I think it's great. Apart from making really juicy reading, it's important that such candid dialogue has been initiated by women about the sometimes outrageous conditions they've had to put up with over their lives.

What I am enjoying most about it is the memory lane it is encouraging women to walk down. For many years I have experienced situations that have made me feel worthless and I've never had an accurate word to file them away under. Well, now I do.

It's been great to know that those awful self-esteem-eroding moments are not mine alone; that women all over the country, for decades, have been living through them, too. That's not to say our lives are a wall-to-wall festival of judgmental and degrading conversations, but occasionally they occur and, man (pardon the pun), are they hard to forget!

One time, early in my radio career, I was told by a male boss that my role was specifically to "be fun, but never funny". The funny bits would be covered by the man I was working with. At the time I was so hurt by this. And also so angry. But I said nothing. Well, technically I did say something, but the conversation was one way, two hours after the meeting, in the car alone, and so filled with expletives it would have made my sugar-cane farmer grandfather blush.

I wanted to tell this guy that in my real life, with my family and friends, I was the funny one. It was so insulting for me, who loved nothing more than making people laugh, to be told that, as a woman, my role was merely to support the man in the show, to laugh at his jokes, but never to "steal his thunder" in the humour department. I was incensed.

Later in my tenure at that job, and after having my first child, I was harassed in my hospital room by phone by the same man.

I didn't want to do a live cross the day after my C-section. I'd haemorrhaged quite badly and gone into shock soon after the birth of my baby, and was riddled with guilt for choosing not to breastfeed. I was in a darkened room with a brand-new baby and frankly trying to process the enormous joy and terror of it all – the baby, the surgery, becoming a parent, and the raging hormones that made me cry ALL THE TIME.

Call me crazy, but I didn't really want to talk about it. Not right then. And yet the calls kept coming. And coming. "The listeners deserve the payoff," he said.

"They've invested in your journey," he said. "This is part of the deal," he said. I couldn't articulate the reasons why I wasn't in the mood, so I did nothing but cry and feel hunted.

Eventually, when I'd been at home for two days, still walking gingerly and changing the dressing on my wound every two hours, I acquiesced and took a call from the fill-in breakfast team, consisting of a former pop star from the '70s and an Olympic athlete and model I'd never met. I stood in my courtyard, so as not to wake my baby, and cried, mobile phone in hand, waiting for the studio to call me for a live cross after the 7.30am news.

With a sniffly voice I answered incredibly personal questions delivered by an impossibly insensitive guest host that included, "How quickly did you start breastfeeding?" ("Ummm ... I haven't") and "How painful was the natural birth?" ("Errr ... actually I had a caesarean"). My partner watched helplessly and angrily from inside. I was deeply and irrevocably humiliated, and we actually never spoke again about this moment.

There are many more examples of times in my working life when I have driven home screaming the lyrics to Moving Pictures' "What About Me" in floods of snot and tears. We all have them, don't we? Is this misogyny? Or is it just gender-non-specific nastiness? Would a male radio host have been put under the same pressure to do a live cross after major abdominal surgery? And if he was, and wasn't up for it, could he have just said, "Nah, mate, don't feel like it," and would that have been the end of it?

I would absolutely have the courage to do that now, but, sadly, sexism preys on the insecure. When I was starting out I would have done anything to keep a job. And that included putting up with the kind of cruelty that would have me charging to the principal's or boss's office if it ever happened to my children at school or at a weekend job.

The saddest thing about all of this is that those women who speak up, particularly at the time of the insult, are labelled "difficult" and are whispered about in boardrooms as candidates for the list of "dames who'll never work in this business again". Because, hey, no one likes a woman who sticks up for herself. Particularly when the attack is fresh.

Thankfully there are now outlets where we can share our terrible episodes and help other women identify that hideous moment when they felt their soul and self-worth was evaporating before their very eyes.

Our work ethic, determination and ability to focus on all the other wonderful men and women we work with makes us all carry on regardless – even if we have to limp for a while. Power to us!

11th November 2012

What DO women want?

I have been stewing over the question: what do women want? For weeks. And I've achieved many things in the lead-up to writing this piece: namely, my house has been cleaned four times, my iPad screen disinfected and polished, two spaghetti sauces have been made from scratch, three bunches of lilies have been trimmed and re-vased, and fourteen loads of little-boy clothes have been neatly folded into piles that rival the sale tables at Seed for neatness and cuteness. I have even invented a brown-rice salad recipe. INVENTED ONE.

All to avoid sitting here, as I do now, and contemplating what it is exactly that women want. I don't want to disappoint anyone here – but, hell, I know many of you will be shocked to realise that this fairly ordinary advertising copywriter turned radio announcer turned TV host, who is currently also a gestating mother of two, does not have the answer.

So stumped was I that I did what any self-respecting researcher would do. I put it out there on Twitter. Now, Roy Morgan I ain't, but the answers I received from other women had a common theme. Grab your highlighter because I'm about to share my findings. And you're not going to want to miss a thing.

In no particular order, what women want is: chocolate and Ryan Gosling. And shoes. And to be able to do a wee without a toddler watching. One woman has a seemingly simple request: for the *Offspring* actor who plays Dr Patrick, Matt Le Nevez, to hunt a bear and then write her a poem about how sad it made him. That can't be too hard, can it? They study bear poetry at NIDA, don't they?

So actors, Mars Bars and bears. Oh my! And here we were thinking this was a complex question that somehow involved equal rights, respect and the frustratingly popular notion of "having it all". How wrong we were!

Is there anything really wrong in believing that a heady combo of confectionery and brooding actors (and bears) is the key to happiness? Does the answer even have to be so cerebral? Most of the women who responded to my question said they actually couldn't possibly answer it. "Too hard," they said. "Changes every day," they said. "When you figure it out, let me know," they said.

A few men even had a crack. Mostly they were of the "who-the-bloody-hell-knows" opinion, but I did have a perplexing exchange with one guy called Jaxzen.

Me: "SO Twitter! What do women want?"

Jaxzen: "It kinda depends on what it is that they want."

Me: "Umm ... yep. That's the question. But thanks for playing, Jaxzen."

Then the real responses came flooding in. Words like "respect" and "love" were pretty popular. "Appreciation" was also big. The more I read, the more I realised that there can never possibly be only one answer.

One woman said what women want is security: not material things, just to be secure in the knowledge that the people in their lives will be there for them.

I liked that.

And these: to be loved and respected.

To do something that matters to someone. To give back and help. And to occasionally be surprised. The crazy lady within me also identified with this: women want both love and space at the same time and a number of other contradictions that make no sense to anyone else but them.

Is anyone confused? And you thought Jaxzen was a worry.

I was lost in a Twittersphere of Louboutins and lollies, kilojoule-free cakes and Christian Grey when I realised there is actually one answer: happiness. That's the goal … What makes women happy is so utterly subjective, but the goal is the same. And surprisingly simple. Women want happiness. But how we all achieve that is up to us.

For some, being able to gorge on chocolate cake and never put on weight will bring the holy grail of happiness. For others, it's all about justice at work and home. Each to their own. Scott on Twitter thinks the answer is "Chicken Dance". Whatever that means.

You know what I want?

I want to be able to have fun wherever I am.

I want to be able to cook with beautiful ingredients always.

I want to laugh. All. The. Time.

I want to have one holiday every year with my family where we have no plans and nowhere else to be.

I want to watch less television and read more books.

I want to be able to whinge about never being able to be alone any more, then, after someone organises a hotel room voucher for me, I want to spend the evening eating chips (that I don't like) from a cylinder and missing my children to the point of tears.

I know that last one doesn't make a huge amount of sense, but I just got the devil in me there ... and I blame Jaxzen.

18th November 2012

Taking stock of the kitchen cupboards

So we are on the move. We sold our house a few months ago, have bought a new one and the removalists have slotted us into their schedules. That sentence rolled off my fingers and onto the keyboard in such an easy fashion it could almost be assumed that the last four months have not been an unmitigated hell. Oh, they have! But they are behind us and we're on our way.

We had most of our life in storage already, but the bits and pieces still in our house had to be moved by someone (that is, me) and frankly I was overwhelmed by the task. The smallest things filled me with anxiety. For example, peering into the fruit bowl, I noticed the contents were: one wizened lime, three bread tags, a toy, twenty-five cents in change, a tube of cold-sore cream, a pacifier (out of action for a year) and two sachets of artificial sweetener.

Not so different from what you'd find in any house, I'm sure. BUT HOW DO YOU PACK THESE THINGS? It made me almost nauseous to realise I had to touch all this ... stuff. All of it. Every piece. I had to touch it and wrap it in something and put it in a box and classify it in some way with a texta word and then move on and touch some more ... stuff. And repeat this exercise until there was no more stuff in the house. Coffee was needed.

Instead, I hatched a plan: I'd go on a throwing-out frenzy. And, given it was garbage night and I had the room to spare in the wheelie bin AND my baby was snoozing, I decided to tackle the pantry first.

Bottom shelf was cans. I gave them a cursory glance and threw out the evaporated milk. I did this because I have recently become friends with some really Italian Italians. They're the real deal. And I'm sorry, but YOU tell them I've toyed with the idea of using evaporated milk in my once-a-year carbonara to save seven grams of fat. And while you're at it, make room in your bed for a horse's head. So tinned milk = gone.

On to the other four shelves, which had been a hotchpotch of categories for the past year or so. It drove my partner mad, but I just couldn't keep any order in there. Even after buying a label writer and 4000 containers with lids, it still looked like something from the TV show *Hoarders.* The first thing I saw were packets of unopened gluten-free crackers and I started to smile. I never expected it but what started as a massive cull ended as a nice walk down memory lane. The gluten-free stage!

Into the green garbage bag went gluten-free crackers, weird yellow penne and a bag of self-raising flour/concrete. I clearly remember buying all that stuff (and more) after reading an article about wheat being evil and making us all fat. Seems the key to staying thin was stocking up on gluten-free food. Because it was inedible. And if you couldn't actually eat your dinner, chances were you were going to come in under your daily kilojoule limit. But, ah, the memories!

Let's move on to the authentic Asian cooking phase, shall we? Healthy! Flavoursome! Hell, there's no reason a chubby white woman couldn't turn out the same food as a seasoned Asian chef! Tucked away at the back of the pantry, I found a significant stash of products that I had originally had to drive a long way to find. Not only that, I had to buy them from people who didn't understand me nor care for my custom. Here was someone who'd watched a doco on Vietnamese street food and thought she was the next Luke Nguyen.

They were right, too. After spending $75 on exotic ingredients, I took sixteen hours to create two bowls of pho. Still smarting, I scowled the next week when I saw someone happily exiting a shop swinging a takeaway bag FULL OF BUCKETS OF PHO for $8. So I opened that garbage bag for the leftover star anise, rock sugar, cassia bark and little squares of muslin. From now on I'd get my pho in a bowl made by someone who had a clue.

Added to that bag were two unopened packets of fried shallots, some Chinese chilli oil (like applying a salve of battery acid and bee venom to my tongue) and a half-used bottle of shao hsing wine (a must-have if you were to recreate *MasterChef* Alvin's drunken chicken – don't pretend you didn't try it, too).

My favourite thing I found was a hexagonal jar of pureed chestnuts and a matching bag of chestnut flour. I decided, as you do, that a chestnut layer cake would be my "thing". And I did make it. Twice. It took four hours each time, and it was unbelievably delicious. The ingredients were so special I could only buy them online direct from the farm that grew the chestnuts. The effort!

Really, this cake was the equivalent of an IVF baby. It was planned. It was wanted. There'd be no mistakes with a chestnut layer cake. And as I took stock of my life – busy busy busy now and busy busy busy on the horizon – I thought, "I'm never going to have the time to spend four hours on a chestnut layer cake ever again."

I couldn't bring myself to bin the pureed chestnut, so I put it back in the pantry. It's now my "aspirational pureed chestnut". I know that when that jar is gone, I will have found either some sanity ... or a single friend with the time to make me that chestnut layer cake.

25th November 2012

The mistakes of Christmas past

Ah, Christmas! There are less than twenty-three days to go and I'm getting a bit excited. I've not done any shopping, nor do I have any actual ideas, but I'm pumped. I actually feel like a seasoned veteran now ... and I will use the experiences I've gained over the past thirty-nine years to make sure that every Christmas from now on is memorable, if not lovely.

We all learn from our mistakes, and when it comes to Christmas, thankfully, we learn from the mistakes of others, too. Sometimes you have to experience those Yuletide lowlights to really make sure you don't repeat them.

For example, the orange and onion salad that appeared front and centre on the trestle table at my great-aunt's Christmas do was the great culinary disaster of 1988. Admittedly, this dish was not made by anyone related to me, by blood or otherwise, and I take some solace in that. An interloper brought it, probably after a conversation that went like this:

Great-aunt: "So we'll see you on Christmas Day then?"

Salad maker: "Yes! What can I bring?"

Great-aunt: "Nothing, we have it all sorted."

Salad maker: "No, really, I know just the thing! I have a salad that will confuse and amaze everyone and leave everyone talking about it until I am long dead! It's inedible and spectacular! See you on the day!"

The setting was a hot Queensland summer and the location was the cleared-out garage under my cousin's house on stilts in suburban Brisbane. The usual suspects were there – a bit of ham, a few cold chooks, some potato salad with Miracle Whip and spring onion. And boiled egg, if I remember rightly.

The temperature was approximately 265 degrees. And in the middle of the table, in a cut-glass bowl, was a salad that I'd never seen before and, frankly, have never seen again. Thin slices of orange and matching slices of brown onion were arranged in an alternating pattern. The dressing? Cream.

Just cream. Orange and onion drenched in cream. This happened twenty-four years ago and I am still confused. I just did a Google search for it and there's no record of it ever being made by anyone, anywhere, in the history of the universe.

I would ask my great-aunt's friend to share the recipe with me, but she's probably no longer with us. Perhaps it was a concoction of mango, cheese and mayo that did her in. Anyway, the moral here is to never serve an orange, onion and cream salad. Anywhere. Ever.

My second tip is to buy stupid, outrageous toys for kids and teenagers that they really want. Not underwear. Underwear is a terrible present for kids. I do not remember the year I got three pairs of Bonds cottontails from my gran for Christmas. No wait, strike that – I do remember because it was every year.

Kids don't want undies. They want stuff like a Fuzzy Pumper Barber & Beauty Shop. Now, I do remember that year. I wept like a baby. It was 1978. I had just turned five. It was the best Christmas ever and before you pooh-pooh the idea of commercial gifts that break, let me remind you that I still have the Fuzzy Pumper Barber & Beauty Shop. I played with it about two weeks ago, totally absorbed in making hairdos out of Play-Doh in my very own barber chair. I am thirty-nine. So there!

One year my sister got a Merlin and she cried, too. Remember Merlin? It would beep a tune and you had to replicate the beeps. From memory. Nowadays it's about as fun as getting a gift-wrapped stick, but in 1981 it was high-tech, let me tell you. We didn't see my sister for weeks afterwards. And when she did eventually emerge from her bedroom with three new pimples and a new bad mood, she only spoke like Dexter from *Perfect Match.* Great gift!

And lastly, make sure you've got the right gift for the right person. One year, my ex gave me a bottle of my "favourite" perfume. Which was actually the scent his ex liked.

I didn't say anything, but every time I wore it we would fight about how boring it was that I was a vegetarian obsessed with *Buffy.* Even though I was, at the time, chowing down on a lamb chop. Amazing how evocative a smell can be. I should've said something, but by the time I'd worn it on a few occasions we'd broken up and that was that.

So there it is. My own tips for a top Christmas? Keep the onion away from the fruit salad; a few rubbishy toys never killed anyone; buy gifts for those you like, not those you despise.

Follow those rules and you can't go wrong. Happy Yule!

2nd December 2012

The best of summer

Everyone has their own definition of what summer means to them. I mean, everyone knows the weather gets hotter and the shirtsleeves get shorter. Most of us will do an inordinate amount of shopping, most of us will have some time off, and nearly all of us will crack open our first lemonade iceblock of the year. But apart from those sorts of things, it's strangely personal the ways in which our behaviour changes in the months from December to February.

Here are the top five things that are synonymous with summer for me:

1. Chafe

Pants are a no-go for me in summer. They're just too hot. But the downside to this is enough friction with each step to light a fire. My thighs seem to resemble sausages the minute I turn that calendar page from November to December. I've actually been tempted to stay up late on November 30 with a torch under my doona so I can watch the metamorphosis as it occurs. I've mentioned this before on my radio show and was quickly put in touch with an underwear company called, ingeniously enough, Chafe Busters. I'm yet to use anything from their range, instead opting for ninety days of walking around like John Wayne from about 2pm each day. Summer is so sexy at my place. Pass me the talc.

2. Mangoes

They start appearing like juicy misshapen eggs a bit before summer and my whole local fruit shop smells of them, so I know they're in season before I can even see them. By December I can buy them by the box, quite cheaply, and my staple diet shifts. It is possible, however, to eat too many, and I've sported mango face-burn and ... errrm ... downstairs-burn, too ... on more than one occasion. I get blasé about them eventually. The first mango of the season is devoured in a kind of ceremony. Slowly and reverently, I slice the cheeks, and score them until I can pop them up from the skin into neat little dewy cubes. The seed gets a good ten minutes of its own. By the end of January, I'm selecting only the ones that are pungent with ripeness and if I get tired of it midway I just cast it off, like Ozzy Osbourne tossing away the body of a bat after he's torn its head off. Next!

3. Hobbit feet

Contrary to popular belief, there are very few freebies in the world of radio and TV any more. However, two years ago I did get a gorgeous pair of very expensive white-and-gold sandals from a photo shoot and I was champing at the bit for the weather to get better so I could give them another run. Last week was the perfect time! So I fossicked into the back of my wardrobe, pushing aside my everyday boots and the pair of wedge heels I wear when I want to emulate a transsexual. I popped the sandals on. Then put them back and toughed it out in my aforementioned boots because ... did someone say Bilbo Baggins? Lurking in my winter boots all year were not actual feet, but instead two cracked and dry-skin-covered paddles resembling feet, with a little bit of chipped nail polish clinging to every second toenail. Note to self: book a pedicure in November every year, and call ahead so their orbital sander is fully charged.

4. Loco children

Nothing sends kids crazier than sudden hot weather that they're not used to. Add to that a bit of daylight-saving action and you've got a surefire recipe for The Bad Seed. My kids are usually bathed, smelling delicious and tucked in by 6.30pm. But in summer? Forget it. On the first super-hot day this year my one-year-old was still toddling around at 9.30pm. Strange sounds came out of his slack little mouth and there was nothing his father or I could do but marvel at how his hitherto straight hair had curled up, and how he had miraculously mastered the arts of clapping, scooting on his bottom and saying "Na na" all at the same time. In the end, we just waited until his batteries ran out.

5. Burns

I am particularly sun-smart. My mother slathered us with sunblock in the '70s, which I'm sure involved ordering the cream from overseas as other Aussie families happily played on the beach completely unprotected, like ants under a magnifying glass. Not us. We had the works. Hats, zinc and 15+, which was the highest you could get in those days. Sure, Mum was using baby oil, but we kids had creamy armour on. So when I talk about burns I don't mean sunburn. I mean burns. In the kitchen. Because I am nude and cooking. The latest spots I'm applying pawpaw ointment to are on my tummy, because I cooked salmon three days ago in the nicky noo-na and some water got in with the olive oil and – BOOM! Splatters of lava-hot oil all over me. Friends, that signalled the end of my career as a bikini model. Which is okay, as I generally swim in the nude as well. Like a plus-size mermaid.

I do love summer. But I reserve the right, after a few hot days in a row, to start whingeing about how I'd kill for a bowl of soup and an open fireplace. And then I'll have another mango and I'll forget I was ever over it in the first place.

9th December 2012

Packing essentials

Here's a tip, from me to you, for nothing. If you have had a huge year, are pregnant with your third child and are lurching towards your Christmas holidays like a cartoon dog in the desert, then here's a piece of advice: do not, at this stage, make arrangements to move house.

I have done this. In fact, I have just done this, last week. And while it's true that I did survive, it was only barely.

Things started to go off the rails when I heeded the advice of a friend and booked the use of "packers". Initially I was in love with the idea. Mainly, because I could say to my colleagues, "Sorry, I just have to take this call from the Packers" and, "The Packers are coming today." Sadly, I was referring to two spry twenty-somethings in matching embroidered polo shirts arriving at the doorstep of my '60s brick veneer and not, as it sounded, organising a lunch date involving lobster and Veuve with an ex-model and a billionaire on a yacht in the harbour. Oh well. Pregnant women shouldn't eat shellfish or drink alcohol anyway, so crisis averted!

The night before the packers were due, I went around the house placing little red tabs on the cupboards I didn't want them to touch.

We still had to live here for six days before The Big Move and I wasn't going to be squatting in my own home. The pantry got a tag, as did my wardrobe. Initially I thought, "What the hell, take all my clothes – I only wear about four things in there on high rotation, anyway." But then I remembered I had stashed a freebie in there that had been sent to me at the radio station that very day.

It was, I blush to reveal, a $220 sex toy. Now, let me get this straight, I wasn't hiding it for use later ... I wanted to show my partner the sheer amazing technology of it and that nowadays these things come with all the bells and whistles. (I stress that's figuratively speaking ... can you imagine?)

Anyway, after we'd laughed nervously about it, turned on each of its SIX SPEEDS and suggested maybe wrapping it up for one of our mothers (ho, ho, ho) I threw it to the back of my top shelf among my trackie daks and old maternity bras. There, it looked about as comfortable as a supermodel at a Weight Watchers meeting. Just as I was contemplating the packers discovering this dirty little secret, I swiftly placed a red tag on the door, mouthing to myself, "I'll deal with our battery-charged friend a little later, methinks." When I arrived home after the packers had gone, I was relieved to find the contents of the wardrobe untouched. The tags worked!

I then filled a drawer in the kitchen with what I considered to be essentials. I'd made a bolognese sauce, so I felt pretty up myself for remembering that I needed to put aside a huge pot and a sieve. I put in some cutlery, about six plates, some plastic bowls for the kids and some glasses and cups. Not exactly a comprehensive list, but enough to cover us for whatever we needed to eat for brekkie, lunch and dinner. My fella, The Chippie, threw in some tongs and a "Barbie Mate" tool. I have no idea why, but I appreciated his effort. So ... I packed that drawer, marked it with a red tag and moved on.

Sadly, for reasons still unknown to me, when I checked the status of that drawer post-packers, I was aghast to find it totally empty. All our essentials ... gone. Somewhere in the towers of boxes stacked high in the living room. It was then I coined the phrase "like trying to find a sieve in a box stack" and you may see fit to use this phrase whenever someone unintentionally, temporarily, ruins your life.

That night we had a roast chicken hacked apart with a butter knife I found in the dishwasher. I peeled potatoes with a little sharp knife, also in the dishwasher. Ever done without a peeler? The potatoes came out looking completely colonial, like something Ned Kelly's lady friend might have prepared the night the Jerilderie Letter was penned. The carrots looked like they'd been whittled with a chisel from a chunk of balsa wood.

My partner and I were on time-share with the solitary fork. I quickly shovelled in my chook, while he paced, checking my plate and asking every few minutes, "How many more mouthfuls are in that for you?" It made me so nervous I got indigestion. Have you ever spied on a cat using the litter tray? Yep. Watch someone do something and they can't perform. In the end I just handed him the fork and said, "Your turn."

Later that night we realised we hadn't planned ahead nearly enough ... my four-year-old's Pillow Pet was packed. As was his night light. The only book left untouched was the boring one about nursery rhymes. And the pull-ups? Gone. Thank goodness for the car boot and its never-ending stash of crap.

So then we were looking down the barrel of five days with almost nothing in the kitchen. I have to say, I enjoyed the challenge. It was like camping, without the insects and digging a hole to go to the toilet.

I'd like to think the moral of this story is that we could all learn to live with less, and that I immediately donated anything I hadn't used in two years to charity, but my lesson was far more superficial. I learnt that peelers are not essential and not to bring home naughty things if you have no intention of using them...

16th December 2012

Living the Christmas dream

There are only two more sleeps to go! I have to admit that I think I may have failed miserably at achieving my dream Christmas. I had all the good intentions of the season but, as usual, I'm pulling it all together at the last minute.

I had grand visions of a stylised Christmas. I do this every year. But I think I may lack an innate sense of, I don't know ... style. Why does my Christmas never look like something out of a magazine?

My Christmas-mad friend has informed me that my first downfall is the lack of a "theme". Hers is "antique silver" this year. She has wooden vessels heaving with glass ornaments, burnished stars in her hallway and a tasteful sprinkling of bright white lights in her garden – solar powered, if you don't mind, because, she says, nothing screams "bogan Christmas!" more than metres and metres of electric cabling. Excuse me while I kick all my cords under the couch.

But, to be honest, I believe I actually do have a theme, although it may not be the focus of a spread in any publication apart from *Hoarder's Weekly*. I believe my concept of "anything goes" is timeless and evergreen, much like the real tree I've been meaning to organise every year. Instead, I have opted at the last minute to just whack up the free fibre-optic one I got once from a store called Kristmas Kingdom. Best gift with purchase, EVER. The great irony is that I bought some Christmas lights from said shop and my cat went to the toilet in the power pack as soon as I opened it. The free tree, however, lives on!

This year, I outsourced the wrapping of every one of my gifts and I highly recommend this. It saves you screaming at your loved ones on Christmas Eve, "GO TO BED SO I CAN DO THINGS!" And this time-planning windfall happened entirely by accident. I did all my shopping in one shop and when the shop assistant blithely asked, "Do you want all these gift-wrapped?" I nearly launched myself over the counter and covered her in yuletide kisses, mistletoe or not.

I went and got a coffee and by the time I had returned everything I had bought was wrapped and trimmed in a way I could never have achieved myself, even with a whole evening in an empty house channelling home-style guru Tonia Todman.

I have made one Christmas resolution that I'm sticking to, though, and that is I'm only cooking or serving or eating delicious things I really like. For years I have squeezed a turkey into my oven, for what? I don't even like turkey. It's dry and weird. And so leggy I feel like I'm dining on Rhonda Burchmore.

But I do like prawns. And I love Moreton Bay bugs. And for 364 days of the year we never eat either. My family and I intend to eat so many of these crustaceans that we'll sprout whiskery things from our jawlines and have our customary afternoon siesta huddled together under a rock, keeping a glossy black eye peeled for predators.

I'm going to have to throw berley in the pool water just to get the kids in there.

There'll be a pumpkin and couscous salad with a yoghurt and mint dressing, something involving potato and bacon and enough pavlova to sink the *Titanic.* Which is a considerable amount, given a pav weighs nothing at all until you digest it and it magically becomes three or four kilos right there on your bottom.

I'm guessing the delicate ballerina who lent her name to this antipodean icon did not ever partake of this dessert, especially the variation involving grated Peppermint Crisp.

I also harbour an unholy penchant for the festive slice called "white Christmas", but every time I eat more than four squares I am plunged into the existential conundrum of what, exactly, is copha? And why does it make me feel carsick? The lion's share of any batch of this mysterious concoction usually hits the bin somewhere around December 28.

I also plan to reprise my annual case of lockjaw from too many Pascall columbines. And have you noticed there are always things that turn up just at Christmas time? I am referring specifically to those Danish biscuits in a blue tin with two tiers of shortbready deliciousness. And panettone. My in-depth research of this phenomenon has revealed that these items are actually "yule-turnal", meaning they come out only when they hear Boney M singing "Feliz Navidad". Speaking of which, Bing Crosby is also yule-turnal. And he is the soundtrack of my day. After a full day of Bing, though, I'm ready to pop him back in the CD case for another year. Ding dong merrily on high, indeed.

I wanted to buy a new frock, but I ran out of time and also, being pregnant, I have no idea what size I am from one minute to the next. What's the next size up from plus-size? Who knows? All I know is that if I can get through the day without my ankles swelling to the size of a yucca trunk it will be a kind of Christmas miracle.

I'm going to go all eco instead and recycle a frock I wore about two months ago. It's black. The colour of mourning. And I suppose I am mourning the loss of my Christmas theme. And the ability to see my feet.

Merry Christmas to all! I'll see you (and my ankles) in the New Year.

23rd December 2012

We are family

I am about three months away from welcoming my third child into the world, and apart from being beside myself with excitement about having what is these days quite a large family, I can't help but think of how lucky this baby is already.

He or she will be born in the same position I was privileged enough to be born into: third. Having two older siblings has been the luckiest stroke of my life and it happened, with no effort from me, on the day I was born.

My older sisters, Catherine and Elizabeth, were nine and seven when I was carried into our outer-suburban home in 1973. I don't remember too much about that house because we moved to the UK soon after, but I hear the eating areas had "revolutionary" carpet. Its main feature was that it could be cleaned by a purpose-built "carpet sweeper", but it could also scrape your shins clean of skin if you fell off your inflatable hopper. It was like you'd come off on gravel.

On the plane to the UK I was looked after by my sisters. They also pushed the Maclaren stroller and later saved up their pocket money to buy me the teddy bear I coveted from Debenhams department store.

Dozens of photos show me sitting comfortably on Catherine's hip, not my mother's. They both always said it was like a dream come true to get a real-life baby to love and look after – and even now, thirty-eight years later, I think they still feel the same. I will always be their baby sister, eternally five, which I'm sure makes it difficult for them to even imagine me with three kids and a mortgage of my own.

Having older sisters gave me an immediate gang. I had two kids who were always on my side. Their influence is a part of my DNA. My parents made my bones, but I feel like those two girls put meat on them.

When I shifted schools in Year 3, I was the only new girl in class. I don't remember having trouble fitting in, but there must have been some issues because Catherine and Elizabeth decided to get me some good press without having to wait for a birthday party.

I wouldn't be ten until November and they simply couldn't wait that long for me to make an impact, so they hatched a plan for an Easter party. And so it happened. All my new friends received handmade invitations in the shape of bunny rabbits and arrived in their Sunday best at my home on a sunny day in March toting armfuls of chocolate rabbits and Humpty Dumpties. I was in with the girls at school nine months ahead of time. Those sisters of mine were PR geniuses!

When all my friends were merely seeing the movie *Never-Ending Story,* I knew the theme song was sung by Limahl – the guy who fronted Kajagoogoo, a group which was the brainchild of Nick Rhodes from Duran Duran. I also knew Limahl's real name was Christopher Hamill and that his stage name was an anagram of his surname.

When my peers were collecting Holly Hobbie, I was collecting imported copies of *Smash Hits* and learning all the words to Nik Kershaw songs. My sisters made me cool. And they got me out of stuff.

I really despised piano lessons, so when it was Catherine's turn to drop me one day I unloaded my gripes on the way. I just loved being in her pale-blue VW Beetle. We would listen to Simple Minds on cassette and enjoy her mixtapes with classics from Grace Jones to Yazoo. When we got to the class she said, "Wait here," and I watched her snake her way, dressed in Staggers jeans and a Saba top, down the side entrance of my cranky, arthritic piano teacher's house. A few moments later she re-emerged and said, with a toss of her Kim Wilde hair, "You don't have to go back. Ever." I think we may have gone and shared a hot chocolate at the Black Cat Cafe instead.

I learnt to drive in Elizabeth's yellow Datsun Stanza. She would take me to a local drive-in car park on Sundays and let me bunny hop as much as I wanted. She never got mad at me for riding the clutch. Later, when she moved overseas, she would write me hilarious aerograms from exotic locations like Tegucigalpa and Cape Town. When she returned one time flush with working-holiday funds, she shouted me an enormously expensive pair of leather boots and I cried because I didn't think I deserved them.

I grew up reading their air-freight copies of *Vanity Fair.* I knew about the photography of Annie Leibovitz and Diane Arbus and the experimental music of Japan, Laurie Anderson and Talking Heads. They encouraged me to read Truman Capote and Harper Lee and Jack Kerouac. And they bought me Swatch watches and Clarins cleansers. Nothing, it seemed, was too good for their "Doll", a name that has stuck with me to this day.

They openly gushed to their friends about my achievements, from class captain to junior librarian, at primary school. They have been delighted by me my whole life. Just delighted. It is a rare gift to know you thrill someone just by your very existence. And they gave that to me freely, constantly. They still give it today.

So to you, my unborn little one who has but three months before you come into this world, I say congratulations. Because you have hit the jackpot with two older brothers who will give you a lifetime of feeling cool and wanted and special. And provide great insight into what a cuckoo lady your mother is!

20th January 2013

Culture shock

When I was eighteen, I took a three-month working holiday to Tokyo. It was the first time I'd felt really conspicuous. Here I was, not able to speak a word of Japanese, trying to negotiate subways and menus and supermarkets, and teaching language to people who couldn't speak a word of English. Let me tell you, this is difficult when neither party understands each other.

More than this, though, was my physical appearance. I felt like I'd walked on to the set of *Gulliver's Travels.* I felt ENORMOUS. At 178 centimetres tall and fairly well rounded, I went the entire time without seeing a single person even vaguely like me. I'd forgotten what this felt like until a few weeks ago, when I moved into the inner city from the 'burbs.

That's right. I'm suffering massive culture shock just eleven kilometres from where I used to live.

Four years ago I moved myself, my partner and my then two-week-old baby to an area with '60s houses on big blocks. We loved it. Sure, it took an age to get to work. It took an age to get anywhere, really, so what happened was we stayed within a tight little radius of our home. We shopped local. We did everything local. And when you get into the swing of all things local, you let your standards slip a bit. I thought nothing of racing up to see Ralph the butcher or Clem the fruiterer still wearing my nightie. I'd check myself in the mirror and think, "Well, this could technically be a singlet dress, and not a nightie, if I just whack on a maternity bra." And I fooled myself like this for almost every day of the four years we lived in our outer-suburban paradise. But we kind of felt like we were missing out on life a bit, so instead of manifesting our midlife crises by way of plug-in hair and small red sports cars, we decided to move to where the groovers are.

I am therefore the daggiest person who has ever resided in our new suburb. Ever. In its history. Which is long.

The first big difference I noticed was the names of the hairdressing businesses. The old neighbourhood was full of places called things like "Shari-Leanne's Salon" and "Snipz on High". Now, my closest hairdresser looks not dissimilar to an IVF lab and is named simply "Blow". Too groovy. I can't go there.

Same for coffee shops. One of our local haunts used to be "Katie's Kafe", but now we sidle up shamefaced for our cappuccinos at places called "Lost" and "The Pound".

Last Friday, I thought I'd slip out and pick up some take away Thai. We had done this regularly at our previous address and it was a shoes optional, park at the door, ten-minute round-trip affair. Not so any more. I ordered our pad thai by phone and headed out the door ... straight into traffic I hadn't seen since grand final day or the Olympics. This is normal? I had to circle the block five times before I could find a park (illegal), and by the time I collected the cold meal I was so stressed I could have used my own sweat as some kind of dipping sauce.

Also, where are the children? In the first week, I said to my partner when we were out with our two little fellas, "It's like that scene from *Chitty Chitty Bang Bang* when the Child Catcher is in town and all the kids are hiding."

Then we rounded a corner and we saw them all! Every child in the postcode playing in a fairly impressive playground because, we guess, their houses might have low-maintenance courtyards instead of yards full of burnt couch grass and bindis, trampolines with cracked mats, and sun-faded Little Tikes para phernalia. Just like our old place had.

It has changed us, though. In a good way. Just this morning, we walked up to the local market and did our shopping with our granny trolley. We got a good takeaway brew and bought organic blueberries and ham off the bone. On the way home I said, "Look at us. Look how hip and inner-city we are!"

As soon as I was in a sidestreet and away from stylish eyes, I had to stop and rest on the aforementioned granny trolley because I was desperate for a loo and my pelvis was starting to hurt. These city fringe areas are not built for women with only two months to go until baby number three. Sensing my discomfort, my man said, "Do you want to push the baby in the pram instead?" To which I replied, "Great idea! It'll be like a walking frame!" (Someone call *Who* magazine immediately and tell them to call off the search for the world's sexiest person, please. I'm right here.)

We do feel plugged in, though. We can hear the rattling of trains and parties on the weekend and we see hipsters riding skateboards home carrying soy lattes. I'm seeing what's "in" and wondering if I could pull off a pair of neon sneakers or a French industrial dining table on casters.

Our kids are seeing different people, too. Brown ones, old ones, poor ones, eccentric ones. Not just wall-to-wall white people in station wagons with kids called Will. I think this is a good thing. It feels new and exciting and real. And it's inspiring me to put on some lippie when I leave the house. And a bra.

Maybe my metamorphosis to full groover will be realised when I have my own wispy little beard and a mini iPad to use exclusively for storing tunes I've heard on community radio stations and while pre-ordering my three-quarter latte? Stay tuned...

27th January 2013

Going crackers for weight loss

How are your New Year's resolutions going a month down the track? Especially the one about trifle-induced kilos? Not good? Fear not – most of us have fallen off that wagon more times than bears thinking about.

If it makes you feel any better, I found a diary from when I was twelve years old and among my resolutions was a commitment to "get skinny". Didn't work. In fact, nothing I've tried has worked. And I've tried more things than you. Trust me.

Firstly, I paid to go to weekly weigh-ins at a major weight-loss cult as a teenager to shed the kilos. Which I did. Mainly through the use of whipped skim milk as a snack. I'd throw half a cup of the stuff into the food processor and after a few seconds I'd have a cup of Nescafé-flavoured fluff. It satisfied me for roughly four minutes then repeated on me so badly I'd foam at the mouth like a distressed snail for the rest of the day. But "nothing tastes as good as skinny feels", remember?

Next came a dodgy doctor. They don't really exist any more – but wow, did they ever set up shop in the early '90s! Admittedly, my "weight-loss specialist" was surprisingly spry for what I imagine was his 178 years. Like Nosferatu, he would seemingly float from room to room, with desperate fat people lining up for an injection of ... something.

Every week I'd show up and bare my ever decreasing bottom for a shot of ... what was that? Horse wee? Who knows, but it made me thinner and I was mad for it. And made mad by it. My bottom still shivers at the memory. I did ask him once what exactly was in the needle and he hissed, "What does it matter? Haven't I made you able to cross your legs like a lady?"

Also, he prescribed something that has now undoubtedly been banned by whatever authority it is that doesn't like people to die. These pills gave me heart palpitations, but in my mania I thought, "So what if I have a heart attack? I'm thinner." Just madness!

I'd take one a day and forget about eating. I could not, however, forget the condition of my mouth as it was as grainy and dry as a Ryvita biscuit and emitted an odour not unlike something you might slip on in an off-leash dog park. I was awake and chattering constantly. I think I shed about twenty kilos in six minutes. And put on twenty-five kilos the minute I went off the mystery injections and banned substance and gave in to a meal consisting of fourteen forms of potato. I remember eating that particular dish like a wolfhound cross who'd been rescued by the RSPCA.

Down the track I joined another weight-loss club which ran meetings in a local church hall. I can't believe what happened here, but it did, and I am sharing it with you now. This organisation was loosely based on the global whipped-milk cult I mentioned earlier and had the most bizarre rituals I've ever come across. And remember, I'm Catholic.

Weekly meetings lasted for two whole hours and went in phases. Phase one was the weigh-in. It's possible I have stood on more sets of scales in my lifetime than anyone in the known universe, so I was essentially unperturbed by this part. But I should've known I'd stepped back in time, or at least entered a Narnia-style wardrobe, when the measurements were in pounds and ounces and the woman who recorded our weights used a quill. A great snack, she said, was cottage cheese and pineapple. On a Savoy cracker. Well lady, let me tell you, I know something here is crackers and it's not the Savoys.

Halfway through the meeting you'd receive your allocation of buttons. Yes, buttons. From the haberdashery. You'd get one for every pound you lost. The first few weeks after I joined I had a severe case of tonsillitis and was so sick I could barely eat, which is usually a terrible thing, except for when you're on a hell-bent mission for buttons.

I wanted those buttons. I was like Gollum for The Ring. I lost something like seven kilos in a fortnight, because I was basically dying, but I got sixteen whole buttons. Now, don't ask what came over me but I went home after those meetings and sewed the buttons onto a green felt bib I was given on joining and wore it every meeting around my neck like a dental patient.

After a month of massive weight loss I had shed more than anyone else and was crowned the Queen of the Club. This involved a ceremony where I stood in front of the entire "congregation" in a long green cloak (no doubt to match my heavily buttoned bib) while carrying a sceptre. Yes, a sceptre. I got to take home a fruit hamper comprising one piece of fruit brought in by every member of the group. I am not kidding.

I just googled to see if these meetings still exist, and they do. In fact, the one in which I was Queen is still going strong. They walk among us, people. Do not be alarmed. And don't forget to bring your bruised banana for the Queen's hamper.

So if your New Year's resolution is to lose weight, do not do as I have done. These days, I walk as much as I can, am teetotal and eat lots of vegies for fun. I am happier. Sure, I'm still heavier than I should be, but I have so much more time to enjoy life now that I don't have to sew on buttons, whip milk or proffer a cheek for a shot of "leg-crosser".

3rd February 2013

The sexist "mummy" label

Have you heard the term "mummy bloggers"? It's a phrase used to describe the clever gang of women who have a little spot on the internet where they write beautifully about the world they live in. Kind of like Virginia Woolf's "room of one's own", but it's a "domain of one's own". In their lovely, intimate space, they create a magnificently rich place where truths are told and lives are exposed in the rawest, most personal ways.

The term "mummy blogger" annoys me. Why? Well ... firstly, why do we have to specify that they're mothers? And secondly, why do we have to do so with the twee word "mummy"? I read many of these blogs – every week, when I get the chance. And these intelligent and creative women write mesmerisingly well about everything from losing partners to suicide and terminal illness to dealing with disability and injustice. Yet the condescending title of "mummy blogger" conversely gives the impression that these online articles deal exclusively with nappies and seven secret ways to use bicarb soda.

The internet has opened up a portal for women who would otherwise not have an outlet to express themselves. Before the advent of the internet, how many women had rich stories to tell – and the ability to tell them with beauty and clarity – but never had the chance? Why do we have to dismiss this important group of writers as "mummy bloggers"? Surely if you write, and people want to read what you write, and seek you out specifically and voluntarily to read what you've written, then you are purely and simply a writer?

Tacking a "mummy" on the front of the term "blogger" somehow diminishes the relevance of those written pieces. Same goes for the excruciating term "mumpreneur". Excuse me – now we have to make up a new, cheesy term for women who have a great idea and make it happen? It's like a little pat on the head, and I want to smack the hand away.

Think of the funky Boost Juice store staffed by gorgeous kids in your local shopping centre. The Boost Juice chain has been a massive success for its founder, Janine Allis. A great idea, brilliantly executed. You've also probably seen a Grill'd outlet as well. Delicious burgers and heavenly fries ... and another example of a wonderful Australian success story for its founder Simon Crowe.

Both of these smarty-pants saw a gap in the market: Allis wanted a good juice so she built a company, and Crowe wanted a good burger so he built a company. Both had to navigate the tricky worlds of finance, marketing, regulations, tax and advertising, among no doubt thousands of others of factors, to steer their companies to ultimate and enviable success. So why is Allis a "mumpreneur" and Crowe a straight-up "entrepreneur"?

If we're to be fair, shouldn't we have "dadpreneurs", too? When was the last time you read about a "dadpreneur"? Or a "manpreneur"? You didn't, because as a society we don't feel the need to categorise the achievements or interests of men in the same way we do for women. By using terms like "mumpreneur'" and "mummy blogger", we downplay the relevance of anything a woman chooses to turn her hand to with any level of success. It has to stop.

And don't get me started on "mummy porn". What on earth is that anyway? From what I can gather – and I'm not a huge consumer of it – "mummy porn" looks a whole lot like the straight-up normal stuff that's been around forever. But when the raunchy book *Fifty Shades of Grey* became a runaway success, it was immediately labelled "mummy porn" simply because the vast majority of people buying it had a set of boozies.

Women love these books. We're mad for them. It made people nervous. It was like someone in a corner office somewhere saw the book's popularity with women and said, "I know! It's written by a woman and mainly women are buying it, so let's whack a 'mummy' on the front of it and make a whole new condescending genre of literature!"

Last year, I was thrilled to be invited to Kirribilli House to hang out with other women for afternoon tea. Prime

Minister Julia Gillard was going to be there too and my dad said, "This is a big deal. You're going." So off I went. Afterwards, it was reported in the media as a meeting between "mummy bloggers" and the PM. Funny thing was, sure, I have children, but I'm not a blogger. At least two other women there had blogs, but didn't have kids. Sure, there were several there who did have blogs and kids, but what difference does that make? It seems now that if you're a woman with a media presence, you're a "mummy blogger" ... such is our desperation to label and categorise.

In protest, I'm going to add the following terms to my everyday lexicon.

Dadoctor: a man who has children and a medical practice.

Hequine vet: a horse specialist who happens to be male.

Manimal handler: an animal handler who is also a man.

Feel free to add your own. And let's see how quickly it catches on.

10th February 2013

Finding the one

This month marks the momentous anniversary of meeting my fella, The Chippie. It was six years ago. I have counted this out on my fingers many times because I can't quite believe how much business we've taken care of in such a short amount of time, as Elvis would say. Three houses, three kids (well, almost) and one trip to "the Worlds" on the Goldie. It's been a very busy time.

When I met The Chippie, I was fresh back from living in regional Queensland for nearly four years. It was summer. I was living with my mum, not working, and had so much free time I was ripe for the pickin'. I'd had a date or two with a man whose name I can't remember and, keen to fill my ample free time, was contemplating pursuing something with him because he was interested and I was bored.

There'd been no kissing. In fact, there'd only been one dinner date where he'd scoffed his dinner, and mine, and then suggested a walk along the beach. In hindsight I can't have been too into him, because I carried my shoes so he couldn't hold my hand and walked at full clip as close to the beach lights as possible so he didn't touch me. Such a goer, me.

Later on, I found out this guy had six toes. I am not a judgmental person, but even I was surprised that an extra phalanx was a deal-breaker. Goodbye, nameless two-dinner eater.

Later that week my friend had a birthday party at a pub, prophetically called The Union, and that was where I first laid eyes on the man who would become my forever sweetheart. Technically he wasn't invited and didn't even know my friend, but a mutual mate had dragged him along for an airing. I love fate. I'm not a mover and a shaker in terms of romance. I've never "picked up" at a pub. But I made sure he had my number, which was a big step for me, and left it up to him.

He was a man, with tools and a ute and a beard, and I got the feeling he'd like to be in charge if anything was to happen. So I waited. Blushing and with heaving bosom, like someone from *Downton Abbey.* And he called. Eventually. And we went out for dinner. It was actually the first time in my life a man had called and asked me out and picked me up for a date. I was so nervous I was moaning to my mum, "I can't go! I'm so boring! I'll bore him to death! He will wish he'd never called!"

But I went and he was adorable. Walking back from dinner, we saw an inconsolable child at an outdoor table of a famous vegetarian restaurant. We both locked eyes on him and Chips muttered, "I think he wanted the steak." That was when I knew.

A few months later we took our first trip away, a week in New Zealand. Perusing a gift shop at

Waitomo, he sidled up to me with a pot of Manuka honey hand moisturiser. "Can you buy this? It'll look weird if I do, being a man and all." So I obliged. I went to the checkout alone and that was when he came up and said loudly, "More beauty products? We're going to need another suitcase for all that stuff you've bought. How much skin do you need to moisturise?" Funny bugger. That was another time I "just knew".

We have never actually had a fight. There have been some very stressful times in our lives over the last six years, including baby-induced sleeplessness, huge decisions with regard to career, selling and moving house and a surprise tax bill that almost sank us. And not once have we turned on each other.

But yesterday St Chippie woke up cranky.

It happens. And I am generally intolerant of crankiness. I think when someone is cranky and I'm in the general vicinity it must be my fault. I take it personally. Also, he may have been checking his iPhone a bit much, which also annoys me – mainly because it highlights my own addiction to Twitter/Facebook/email/random Google searches.

He was sitting outside while I was cleaning the kitchen, a combo that tests me. Okay, sure, he was supervising the kids, ostensibly making sure that our one-year-old's daily fibre intake didn't consist entirely of sand, but still ... to me it looked like I was doing something tedious and he was not. Not fair! And he was on his phone. Again. Characteristically keen to not mind my own business, I shouted from the sink, "What on earth are you looking at on that damned phone?"

And that was when Dr Hook's "When You're in Love with a Beautiful Woman" started blaring from our speakers. Knowing that he's a lover of gadgets and music, I'd bought him a whizbang thing for Christmas – a speaker that remotely accesses every song you have on iTunes via mobile phone and plays it from your phone – no cords. It's a miracle I have yet to fully comprehend because my handle on how technology works expired in 1993 with the mystery of the fax machine.

How can you stay mad when someone is playing your song? You can't. Now smiling, I waited for more of his "make Chrissie happy" playlist and out they trotted – "Knowing Me, Knowing You" by ABBA, "Guilty" by Barbra Streisand, "River" by Joni Mitchell – each made even sweeter because I know he'd rather pass a kidney stone than listen to them. As I happily sprayed and wiped, singing along to "Crazy in Love", I realised that even six years down the track I could have another "I just knew" moment. So here's to fate and bearded Chippies and "Rio" by Duran Duran.

17th February 2013

Baby talk

It's hard not to talk about your kids incessantly. In fact, when you have just one, it's damned near impossible.

I remember when I had just one, my first, Leo, in 2008; I talked of nothing else. I was working in breakfast radio, so I had the kind of outlet every first-time mother craves: a microphone, listeners who can't tell you to shut up and a quote I'd read somewhere that said "babies are good for ratings". A heady combo.

When Leo was about six months old, I stumbled across a forum on the radio website. (Okay. I didn't really stumble across it. I logged on and searched for entries with "Chrissie Swan" in the title. I believe they call it a "vanity search" these days. I also believe it was the last time I ever googled myself.)

If I'd received a dollar for every time the sentiment of "would she just STOP banging on about her bloody baby" was expressed I'd be writing this column from a yacht moored off the Bahamas, drinking diamonds out of a platinum straw. It was then that I realised that incessant chatter about your child is interesting to a very narrow demographic of, well, you. And maybe your mum. That's it.

Something eventually happens to most people to stem the flow of first-baby banter – usually the far less life-changing birth of a second child – but until then, first-time parents have no idea how boring they can be. Bless 'em.

I was at a bon voyage shindig last week for a friend who's moving interstate. There was a producer here, a gay man there, a young bearded stand-up comedian mixing mojitos and the inner-city neighbour with, you guessed it, one toddler sleeping next door under the watchful gaze of Grandma.

Admittedly, with such a diverse group of strangers it's hard to find a topic common to all. But let me go out on a limb here and suggest that the winning subject is probably not mothers' group. I've been so embarrassed by my own self-absorbed baby talk that as soon as I get a sniff of it I panic and try to steer the conversation somewhere else – anywhere else. I end up treating the whole conversation as if I'm one of those dodgem car supervisors: the baby talker is on the track, going the wrong way, ruining the fun for everyone, and I'm perched on the back of the car, leaning over the errant driver and taking control of the wheel. More often than not, the driver lasts a few minutes on their own in the right direction and then, boom, wrong way and I'm on the dodgem again.

At the aforementioned party, this poor woman kept on about the trials and tribulations of mothers' group to a woman who hadn't been in one for thirty-five years, a woman who'd once been in one for a week (me), one man who'd never had kids and another who was a gorgeous 21-year-old and was no doubt living in a prophylactic seven days a week.

She may as well have been floating the concept of bonobos and their penchant for flash cards. No one could play along. And no one really cared. I'm pleased to say I was able to steer the conversation, dodgem-style, to the groundbreaking TV show *Embarrassing Bodies* and everyone could squirm together and attempt to answer such questions as, "If you've been so embarrassed by the skin tag on your bottom for twenty-five years, why do you suddenly break your silence, complete with telescopic camera footage, on a show seen by, I don't know, the entire world?"

Having a child was completely life-changing for me. It has been the best thing I've ever done. I know it sounds corny, but I felt it gave me a purpose that I didn't even know I'd been lacking. I love it. That's why I'm doing it again. And might even contemplate doing it a fourth time. I'm crazy like that.

But that's my story and there's a limit to the discussions you can have about all that stuff, and especially the audience you can have them with. An anecdote is fine. Go for it. I feel no guilt when sharing in mixed company that my four-year-old asks hilarious and dumbfounding questions such as "Why do we need a forehead?" and "Why does Spider-Man do whatever a spider can?" But a guessing game at a barbecue centred around "What percentile do you think little Jimmy's head circumference is in?" is just bad manners. Same goes for statements like, "I really thought Jemima would be twelve kilos at her maternal health check-up, but she's 13.3!"

I know it sounds harsh, but who cares?

It is a tough day when you realise that the vast majority of people you meet don't really care about your stories of breast pumps, which mattress is best, rapid out-growing of Wondersuits and how much stain remover you have to use on the shoulders of your clothing to remove those foamy spit stains. You might even be angry at me for suggesting it, as I absolutely was at User6789 on that radio forum page who wrote, and I quote, "If I hear the words 'my baby Leo' one more time from Chrissie Swan I swear I will voluntarily fill my ear canals with molten lava."

I'm not saying don't talk about it. I'm just saying it's probably best to write it down instead, for the exclusive pleasure of the one person who will really dig it, starting with the words "Dear Diary". You'll thank me. Eventually. I think. (*retreats sheepishly*)

24th February 2013

Rubbed the wrong way

I haven't had the best luck with massages and the like. The first time I ever disrobed (for a stranger I hadn't met on an internet dating site), I was in Bali on a holiday my mum had shouted me. I was in my mid-twenties, we were staying at The Village of Enchantment and had heard all about this amazing place that did "THE BEST MASSAGES". So off we went.

Upon arriving at the place we were presented with a menu of services. Having no idea what was what, I just went with the Full Body Massage. Excited to be finally getting into something everyone had been telling me about for years, I was led to a private room by a tiny woman in a mint-green uniform. Let's call her The Assailant. She suggested, in broken English, I get my gear off, and she'd be back in a minute.

I should've hailed a cab at that point. But didn't. And that's why I can write this column for you today. I got naked and immediately was struck by how deeply I did not want my immense body to be touched all over by a small and obligated Indonesian woman while I was in the nudie-rudie. Didn't want it. Not one bit. But did I say so? No. I went along with it, because, hey, I was already naked and there were frangipanis in the bath and didn't everyone just love full body massages?!

So I endured the massage and it hurt. A lot. I don't know about you, but I don't hold a lot of tension in my shin bones and last time I checked it really hurts when someone drags their knuckles across them. I think I blocked out the rest of it and loved it when she intimated that it was over and I should relax in the bath. I hopped in and as she left I just felt relief.

I was covered in burgeoning bruises and, frankly, had the previous forty-five minutes occurred anywhere else, it would have been deemed an assault. But at least I was alive (barely) and I'd learnt a valuable lesson – I'd never need another full body massage. In. My. Life.

My relief was short-lived. About seven minutes later, my tormentor returned and motioned for me to get out of the bath. The bath was sunken, so I got out of it with approximately the same amount of grace as a foal being born. I then sat opposite The Assailant, like a huge, hot, naked, embarrassed beanbag, and allowed her to rub moisturiser into my boozies. I cannot explain why I didn't just get up and leave.

I'll never know. I only offer to you, dear reader, that this "suffer in silence" mentality is hereditary and I got it from my mother.

My mother, while on holiday interstate, was talked into a massage at a bathhouse. She'd had a tricky hip and a friend, or maybe it was my sister, had recommended this wonderful man who could fix it in a jiff. She got her clothes off and waited for this hip magician to materialise. When he did, he looked less like a miracle masseur and more like a small Asian man who didn't speak English. Mum tried to explain that her hip was very painful. He didn't understand. Eventually she pointed to her groin region and started nodding furiously. She then made it worse by clasping her hands together in the universal symbol for pleading. He misunderstood. REALLY BADLY.

The groin, the nodding, the pleading.

It went a bad way very quickly and an English-speaking supervisor was called to diffuse the situation with the randy old lady in treatment room Number 5.

Mortified? Sure. But Mum didn't grab her stuff and leave. She went through with the massage, even though he was rough and she was almost dying from the pain.

Three days later I picked her up from the airport. I watched as hundreds of people snaked out of the plane, until only the flight attendants were dribbling out. Then there she was, last off, in a wheelchair. She hadn't mentioned it to me! And she hadn't mentioned it to the guy who had dislocated her hip, which he no doubt did while thinking, "That'll teach you for hitting on a masseur, lady."

I'm three weeks away from baby number three and yesterday, as I dragged myself into the upright position at 4am to get ready for my radio job, I actually heard my body make a noise I'd never heard it make before. It was exactly like the sound I'd imagine the hull of the *Batavia* made moments before it was wrecked at sea. I am like a giant creaky boat. But I will not get a massage. No, sirree.

I also have a unique and wonderful condition called pubic symphysis diastasis. I call it "hammer hoo-hoo" because essentially it feels like someone has just gone through my pubic bone with a hammer. In fact, just last week I reviewed that title and have now escalated it to "axe hoo-hoo". I can't walk further than twenty metres without searing pain. I would seriously like a Zimmer frame. But will I get a massage? No. I will not.

All of this physical misery will be alleviated when the baby is born – in twenty or so days. And I can live with the physical pain of axe hoo-hoo for the next twenty days, rather than the lifelong humiliation I can imagine will ensue if I make an appointment for someone to alleviate any pain centred around my private bathing-suit area.

No thanks. I don't want to end up in a wheelchair. I'm happy creaking.

3rd March 2013

Turning forty

I am turning forty in a few months and it doesn't faze me one little bit. I have several friends who are also hitting this milestone at around the same time, and they are split fifty-fifty between those who couldn't care less (like me) and those who shiver like a nervous Pomeranian left outside a supermarket at the mere mention of it. I'm thrilled with where I am at forty. In love, with three extraordinary children, a fabulous career and a home I plan on staying in for so long that I'm imagining where the ramps will go. Things are good. Sure, I'm also feeling old. But in a good way. Old like Dame Judi Dench (read: sage), not old like Jackie Stallone (read: ouch).

My thirties have been mayhem, and I am hoping my forties will be just as busy, but, to be honest, not as physically taxing. I have worked a lot and grown a lot of humans in the last five years, and I am looking forward to retiring my soft trapdoor maternity bras and sleeping without a night light. And yet I know that when those moments come, I will be so very sad about them.

I am also looking forward to having sex again. One day. You know what they say ... naughty forty! Allegedly. We'll see.

Anyway, a person can learn a lot in forty years. So, here I give you the things I know for sure after forty years on this planet:

Nothing says, "Welcome home, I love you," more than being able to sniff a cooking free-range chook or beef bourguignon all the way from the driveway.

Making a commitment to eating a breakfast of quinoa, almond milk and pomegranate seeds every single day is not sustainable when egg-and-bacon toasties are still available in the world.

"Nesting" is a twee word for the biological compulsion to purchase useless things while you're pregnant. Also, is anyone keen on a pair of oriental-themed bedside tables, sixteen cushions made from vintage tea towels, or a yoghurt maker? Going cheap.

Avoid the hairdresser while pregnant or newly at home with a baby. You will leave the salon looking like a cockatoo or Brian Mannix in the "Everybody Wants to Work" film clip, circa 1984.

Stevie Nicks from Fleetwood Mac does a much better show when she's clean and sober. I say this after seeing her perform, many years ago, to a packed and somewhat shocked arena, while remaining mostly horizontal on what appeared to be a bed of incense, handkerchiefs and tambourines.

Heaping over-the-top praise on your children for no reason is absolutely fine. I regularly look into my four-year-old's eyes and tell him he is the most perfect, clever, funny and beautiful human being who ever walked the earth. He quakes with pleasure. I figure he won't care that I am working hard to give him a great education and organic bananas, but I hope he will remember my face looking at his and telling him he is amazing.

Either decide to leave your bikini line in its natural state or commit to seeing a professional waxer regularly. It's one or the other. Trust me, I've tried DIY and ended up with a pelt not dissimilar to that of an itchy Balinese street dog. Ignore this warning at your own peril. But if you do, my friend Clementine and I suggest that a Mason Pearson hairbrush will give you the best relief.

Working doesn't make you a bad mother. And staying at home doesn't either.

If someone is eyeballing you while you physically fill out your details on any kind of form, you will never, ever be able to remember the date. And, usually, you will forget what year it is too.

Being punched in the face will hurt a lot less than if your kid says, "You never play with me."

Peter Allen's "Tenterfield Saddler" is the saddest song ever written.

Sometimes, kids just want to watch *The Super Hero Squad Show* with a glass of milk instead of exploring role-play via Play-Doh sausages. You are not a bogan for letting them.

Try to throw out fresh-cut flowers before the water in the vase starts smelling like the kind of place inhabited solely by boiled eggs, discarded big toenails and Gollum from *The Lord of the Rings.*

And lastly ... I don't think women can "have it all". I just realised this right now. How do I know? I work in the morning and that means I can't drop my kids at kindergarten or, when the time comes, school, even though I would dearly love to. On the other hand, my friend, who stays at home with her kids, sometimes calls me in desperation just to remind herself of what a person taller than three and a half feet sounds like. There. In two simple, logical examples I have proven women can't have it all. If that's what "all" means. So stop asking the world's most stupid question already.

I could go on ... but I have a party to plan. I'm inviting everyone who's made me laugh during the last forty years. I'd better warn the neighbours.

12th August 2013

Acknowledgements

Knowing that this might be the only time I got to write one of these, I really wanted to put a lot of thought into it. Then *Geordie Shore* came on TV and I had to defrost a lasagne and the deadline was two hours ago so I'm just going to whack all these wonderful, inspirational, patient and helpful people in the list below.

You know what you've done.

And you know I think you are awesome.

Kate Cox, Pat Ingram, Danielle Teutsch, Caitin Yates, Jeanne Ryckmans, David Wilson, Andrew Gaul, Robyn Cornell, David Vodicka, Yasmin Naghavi, Kirsty Webb and Jenn Dutton.

A special thanks to my amazing parents, Pat and Garry Swan, and my spectacular sisters, Catherine and Elizabeth Swan. The gift of your company, humour and insight has been the highlight of my first 40 years.

And to my diamond. Chris Saville. Aka The Chippie. Thank you for bringing my carefree twenties to an end in the most wonderful way possible. And for making me feel good about every little thing. She loves you.

PHOTO: MARK LOBO

CHRISSIE SWAN is a broadcaster and TV personality. She was host of the Network 10 programs *The Circle* and *Can of Worms* and the MIX 101.1 radio programs 'Chrissie and Jane Breakfast' (Melbourne) and 'The 3pm Pick-Up' (national). In 2015, she was a contestant on *I'm A Celebrity ... Get Me Out of Here!* and a columnist for the weekend *Herald Sun.* Follow Chrissie on Twitter @ChrissieSwan

Chrissie Swan is personally managed by David Wilson at Watercooler Talent & Media: www.watercooler.net. au; @watercoolertwit.

Back Cover Material

You know what I want?

I want to be able to have fun wherever I am.

I want to laugh. All. The. Time.

I want to have one holiday every year with my family where we have no plans and nowhere else to be.

I want to watch less television and read more books.

I want to be able to whinge about never being able to be alone any more, then, after someone organises a hotel room voucher for me, I want to spend the evening eating chips (that I don't like) from a cylinder and missing my children to the point of tears.

From weight to wee, children to crap dates, nothing is off limits for Chrissie Swan, self-confessed 'over-sharer'. Celebrity, friendship, love, being a working mum, 'having it all' and the general chaos of life – *Is It Just Me?* is Chrissie at her hilarious, candid and fearless best.

'Smart, sassy, funny. Chrissie is the best girlfriend everyone should have. And with this book, now they can.'
MATT PRESTON